The TREE ALMANAC

A Year-Round Activity Guide

MONICA RUSSO

Photographs by Kevin Byron

Sterling Publishing Co., Inc. New York

Edited with layout
designed by Jeanette Green

Library of Congress Cataloging-in-Publication Data

Russo, Monica.
The tree almanac : a year-round activity guide / by Monica Russo : photographs by Kevin Byron.
p. cm.
Includes index.
Summary: An introduction to trees through the seasons. Suggests activities.
ISBN 0-8069-1252-9
1. Trees—Juvenile literature. 2. Seasons—Juvenile literature. 3. Botany—Study and teaching—Activity programs—Juvenile literature. [1. Trees. 2. Seasons.] I. Byron, Kevin, ill. II. Title.
QK475.8.R885 1993
582.16—dc20 92-41347
CIP
AC

2 4 6 8 10 9 7 5 3 1

First paperback edition published in 1994 by
Sterling Publishing Company, Inc.
387 Park Avenue South, New York, N.Y. 10016

Distributed in Canada by Sterling Publishing
℅ Canadian Manda Group, P.O. Box 920, Station U
Toronto, Ontario, Canada M8Z 5P9
Distributed in Great Britain and Europe by Cassell PLC
Villiers House, 41/47 Strand, London WC2N 5JE, England
Distributed in Australia by Capricorn Link (Australia) Pty Ltd.
P.O. Box 6651, Baulkham Hills, Business Centre, NSW 2153, Australia
Manufactured in the United States of America

Sterling ISBN 0-8069-1252-9 Trade
0-8069-1253-7 Paper

Adult supervision is always recommended for children doing unfamiliar science or craft projects. Also heed the caution about poison sumac that may grow in your area.

Dedication

This book is dedicated to my mom and dad, who planted many kinds of trees over the years—dogwood, plum, birch, maple, and hemlock trees, to name just a few. Today these beautiful trees are living time machines, providing memories of the past, while growing with us into the future.

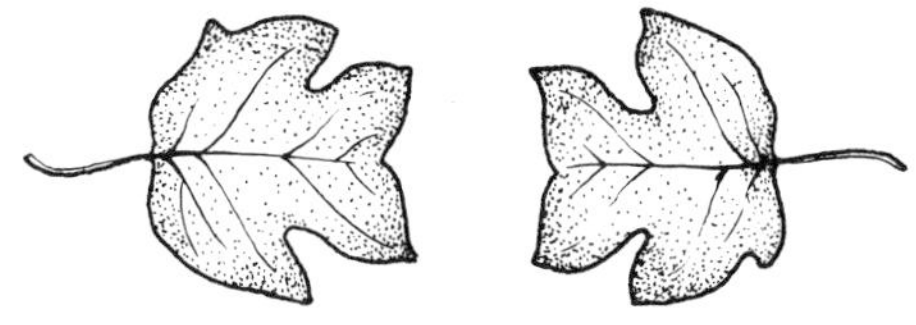

Contents

Author's Note 7

1 What Is a Tree? 9

What Is a Tree? 9
Leaves 10
Wood—the Inside Story 13
The Living Tree 15
Tree Science 17
Record Setters 22
Old-Timers 25

Hands Off! 27

2 Spring 29

Maple Sugar Time 29
Big, Beautiful Blossoms 31
Celebrate Spring! 42
Look for New Growth 46

3 Summer 47

Battle against Bugs 47
Scouting for Trees 49
Identifying Summer Leaves 53
Looking at Trees from around the World 63

4 **Fall** 69

Losers Win 69
Star Attractions 73
Falling Leaves 77
Time to Investigate 80
Autumn Harvest 81
Food for All 88

5 **Winter** 93

Evergreens 93
The Survivors 103
Winter Activities 104
Be a Budding Botanist 107

6 **Trees for People and People for Trees** 113

Tree Families 116

Tree Terms 122

Index 126

Trees, Glorious Trees *color photos follow page 64.*

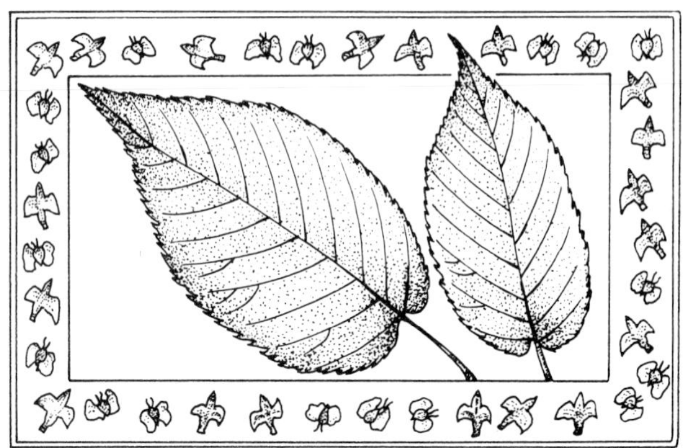

Black birch with border of birch seeds

Author's Note

The trees around our log cabin were the models for many of the photos and drawings used in this book. We also used trees in parks, backyards, roadsides, and nature trails in Maine and other states. Pressed leaves and dried herbarium specimens were invaluable to creating many of the drawings.

Kevin Byron has photographed trees through all seasons for many years. He has taken shots while hiking more than 10,000 feet up in the Rocky Mountains, has sloshed through red maple swamps amidst mosquitoes and black flies, climbed fire towers, and visited apple orchards to get the photos used in this book.

Many people were generous in their assistance, including state forestry employees and paper company agents. Our thanks also go heartily to the Strauchen family who gave us an unparalleled opportunity to study the flora and fauna of northern Utah; to Moody's Nursery in Saco, Maine, where Kevin shot close-ups of the saucer magnolia; and to the Legros family, who let us tramp around their wonderful Maine woodlot to get pictures of their tapped maples. We thank Tri-Town Publishing in Dover, New Hampshire, for letting us reprint Kevin's picture of the great horned owl. My appreciation is also extended to Sheila Barry and Jeanette Green at Sterling, for their guidance in the cultivation of *The Tree Almanac*, so that each leaf of the book offers discovery to the reader.

Magazine and newspaper articles were carefully researched, along with classic textbooks more than 100 years old, including books by famous botanists such as Liberty Hyde Bailey and Asa Gray. An enormous variety of field guides, trail guides, technical reports, and botanical textbooks were also studied.

Most of all, I thank my parents for their lifelong enthusiasm in planting trees and shrubs, observing the environment, and providing a fascinating sanctuary in which to study all aspects of nature.

Monica Russo

This eastern white pine seedling may grow as tall as 80 or 100 feet (24 to 30 m).

1

What Is a Tree?

What Is a Tree?

All trees are **plants**, and most trees have these features or traits.

They grow at least 15 feet (4.5 m) tall.

They can live for many years—sometimes hundreds or even thousands of years.

There is usually one main trunk, protected with a hard, tough bark.

Trees have a "crown" of leaves.

It's easy to identify plants that are *not* trees, like grass, mushrooms, or ferns. Flowers like tulips, daisies, and roses aren't trees, either. Even woody vines with bark on them, such as grape vines, aren't trees.

Short Stuff

Woody shrubs or bushes like lilac, blueberry, or azalea aren't trees, because they don't grow tall enough. They usually grow from a clump of many stems, instead of one main trunk.

Parts of a Tree

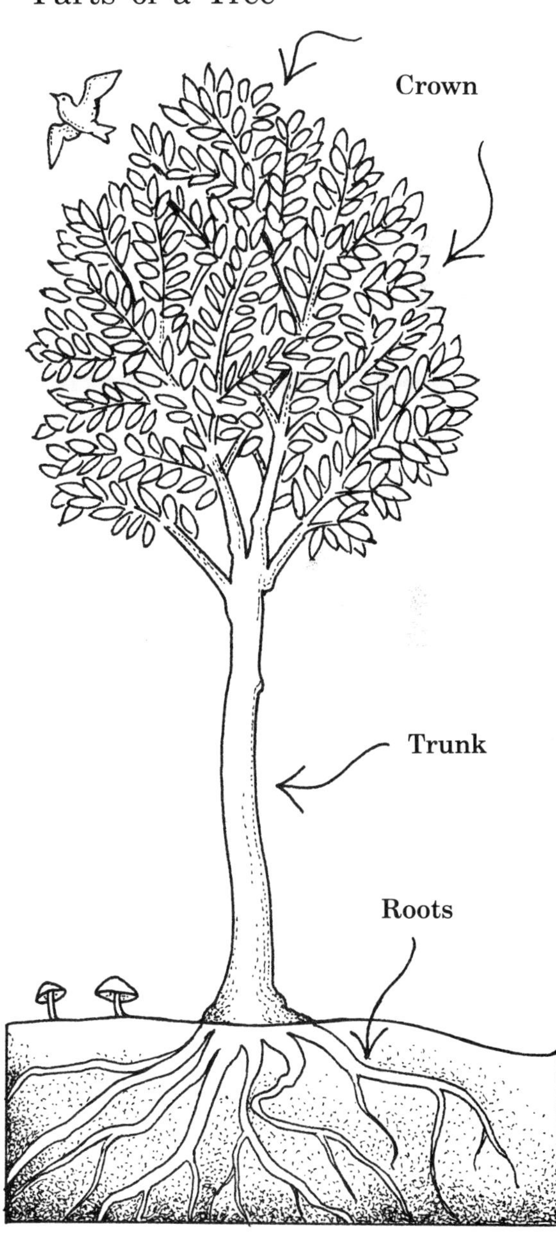

Shrubs and bushes aren't trees, since they don't grow more than 15 feet (4.5 m) tall.

Some trees are kept short by trimming or pruning, so they look like shrubs instead. An **apple tree** can grow as high as 30 feet (9 m), but most apple trees are pruned to keep them much smaller. An **eastern hemlock tree** growing in the forest can reach 75 feet (22.5 m) tall. But this tree can also be trimmed to make a hedge that's only a few feet high.

The Parts of a Tree

Most trees have three main parts.

Crown Branches, twigs, leaves, buds, flowers, and sometimes fruit.

Trunk Usually very thick and growing straight upward.

Roots Big roots branch into smaller and smaller roots until they are tiny and as fine as hairs.

Form and Shape

The shape of the leafy crown is different for the different types of trees. **Fir trees** and **spruce trees** have a pointed, triangular shape. **Maple trees** have rounded crowns. The crown of leaves on many **palm trees** looks like a clump of big feathers.

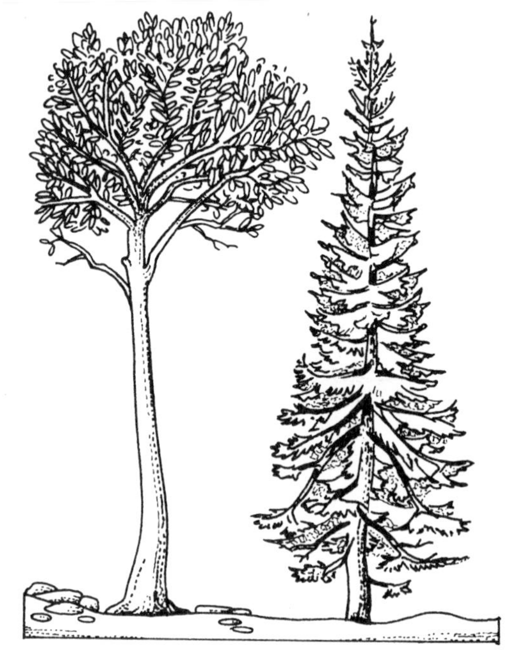

A red maple has a rounded crown of leaves, but a balsam fir has a pointed crown, with branches close to the ground.

Leaves

Most trees can be identified just by their leaves. Tree leaves have many different shapes—oval, heart, triangle, or very thin and needle-like. Some leaves have smooth edges, but others have jagged teeth.

Here are some different shapes of tree leaves.

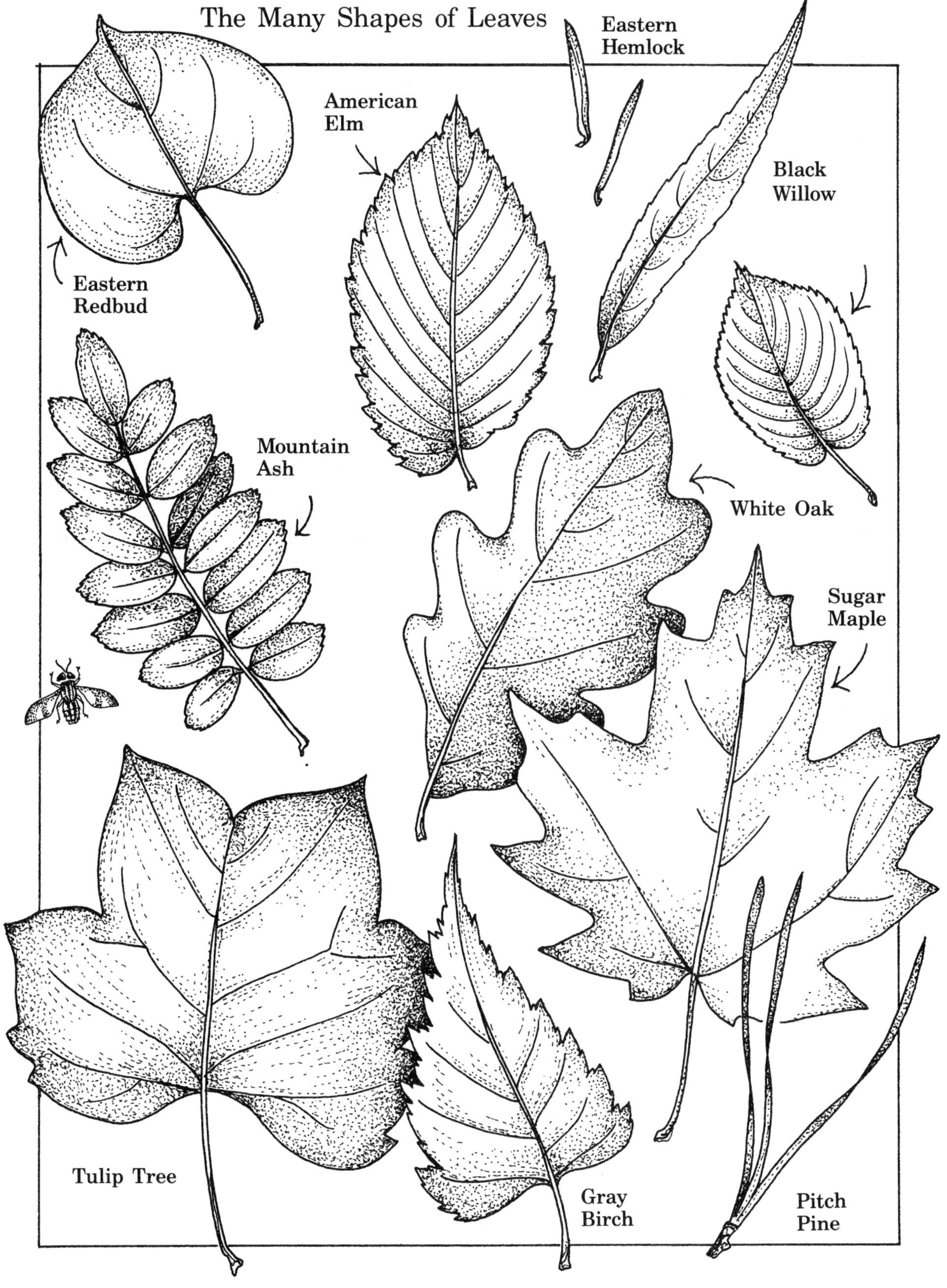
The Many Shapes of Leaves
Eastern Hemlock
American Elm
Black Willow
Eastern Redbud
Mountain Ash
White Oak
Sugar Maple
Tulip Tree
Gray Birch
Pitch Pine

Parts of a Leaf

A leaf has three main parts.

Petiole It's also called the leaf stem. It can be long or short, thin, thick, or flattened.

Blade The flat, green part of the leaf.

Leaf Veins A pattern of ribs or grooves that can look like a complicated web or a network of roads.

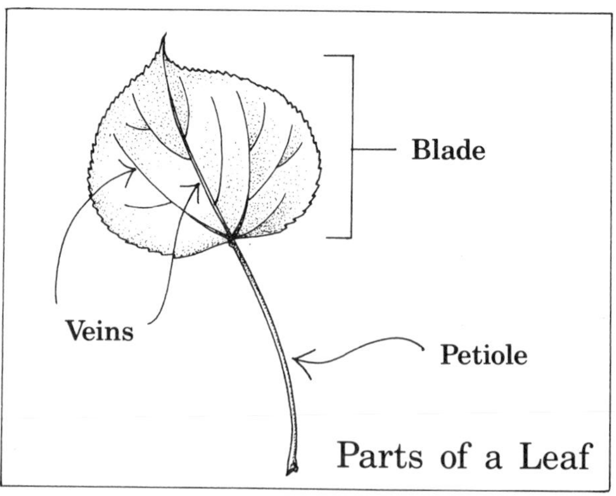

Parts of a Leaf

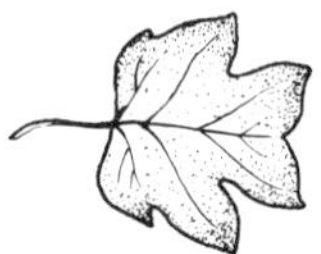

Noticing how the leaf is shaped or how the veins are arranged will help you match a leaf with a picture in this book, or in any field guide. And you'll soon learn the name of the tree.

By looking at the leaves, you'll be able to identify many of the trees growing around your school, town park, or near your house.

The needle-like leaves of this blue spruce *are stiff and sharply pointed.*

Wood—the Inside Story

When a tree is cut down for lumber, or to be burned as fuel, you can see the inside wood of the trunk.

Here's what a tree trunk cut straight across would look like.

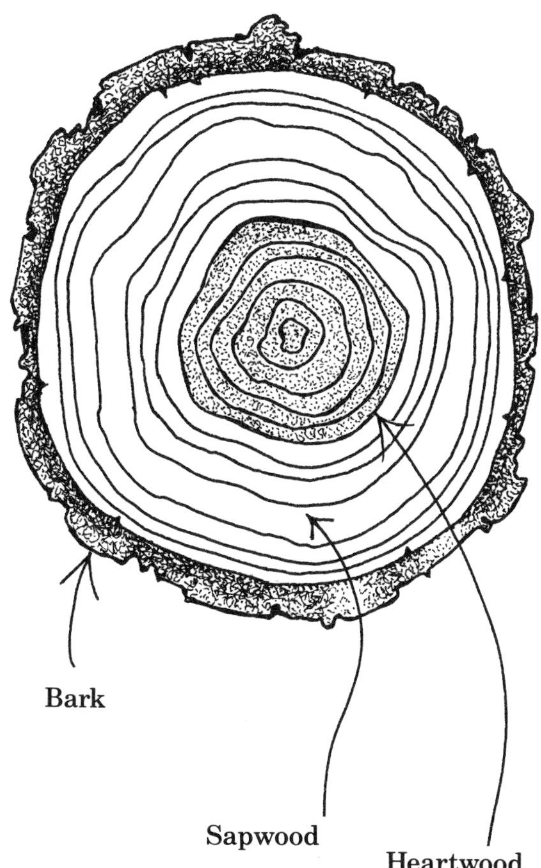

Parts of a Tree Trunk

U.S. dollar bills are not *made from trees or wood pulp, but from a small flowering plant called flax.*

Bark

This can be scaly, grooved, rough, or smooth. The bark protects the inside of the tree from drying out, from insects, from cold, and from some diseases.

The bark of a few species of tree is very distinctive. The bark of a large **American beech** is smooth and light grey, and has tempted many people to carve their names in it. This can affect the health of the tree, since insects or diseases can work their way inside.

The white, chalky bark of the **paper birch** and other birches can be peeled away from the trunk, and has been used as writing paper. In Canada in the early 1900s, people travelling north even sent birch-bark messages back home as postcards or letters!

You can try to write or draw on birch bark peeled from fallen logs or cut wood. But *don't* peel bark from living, standing trees, since removing the bark would harm the health of the birch.

Sapwood

This is the growing part of the tree, and it is usually light in color. Circles called **growth rings** (or annual

*You can count the annual growth rings from the center outward on this **white oak** to find out its approximate age when cut down.*

rings) show how much the tree has grown in a year. A new layer of **sapwood** is formed each year, and each layer makes another ring. If you count all the rings from the center outward, you'll know how many years old the tree is.

A plank of **lumber** shows the growth rings from a long side view. The long lines, or **grain**, of the lumber is really the pattern of the growth rings. Grain looks different for different types of trees.

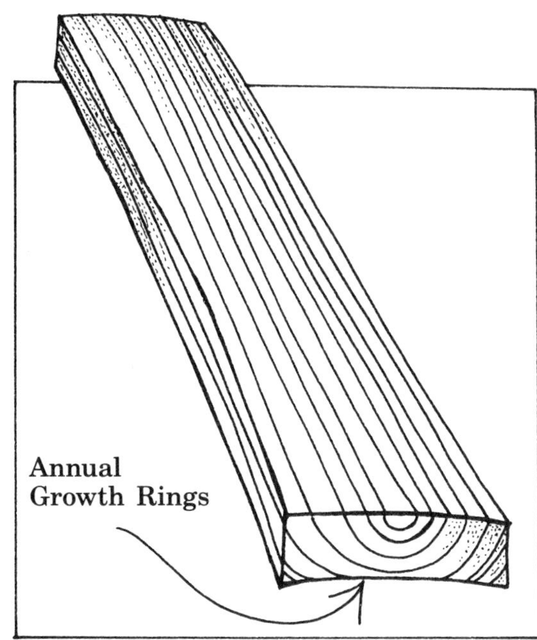

The pattern of grain on a plank of lumber is made by the growth rings.

Heartwood

Heartwood is at the center of the trunk. In some types of trees, like **redwood, black walnut,** and **hickory,** the heartwood is much darker than the sapwood.

Heartwood from **western red cedar** and **redwood** is resistant to decay and rot. So, lumber made from the heartwood of these trees is more valuable than other types of wood.

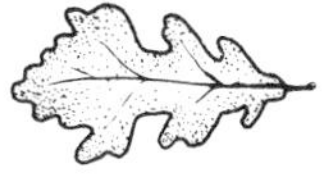

Heavy or Light?

Some wood and lumber weighs more than others. A plank of **white pine** lumber weighs a lot less than a plank of **red oak**. The wood and lumber of the pine is also softer. And it is easier to cut or carve.

The Living Tree

Photo what?

Photo*synthesis*. Without living plants, there would probably be no animal life on Earth. That's because plants produce **oxygen,** a gas which animals need to breathe. Trees and other plants need certain things to make oxygen.

Water From soil dampened by rain, streams, or swamps, and from fog and mist

Light From the sun

Carbon Dioxide A gas which animals (including people) breathe out

Drops from a spring shower hang on the twigs of this wild raisin tree. All trees need water to live.

At the same time that oxygen is being made, the plant also makes a kind of sugar to use as food. The process of combining water, sunlight, and carbon dioxide to make oxygen and sugar is called:

Photosynthesis

(foto SIN tha sis)

Water Works

The roots of a tree collect **nutrients** from the soil and also **water.** More water is absorbed than the tree actually needs. This extra water is moved upward to the leaves and then evaporates back into the air. Growing, living trees are constantly putting water into the air, where it becomes cloud vapor and rain.

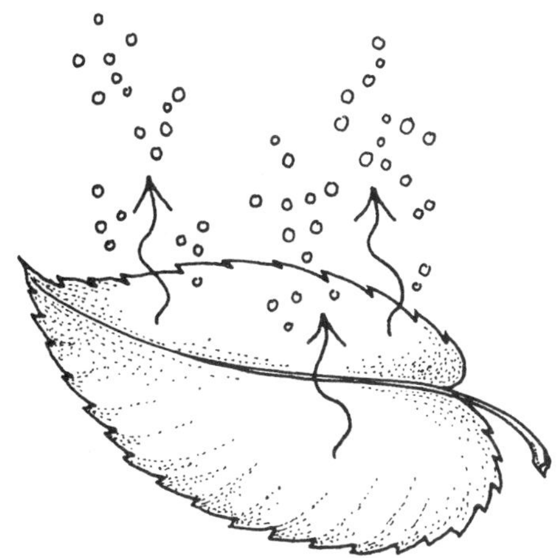

Microscopic droplets of water evaporate from tree leaves back into the air.

A champion-size American beech grows in Maryland. It's about 130 feet tall!

Tree Science

Who Studies Trees?

A scientist who studies plants is called a **botanist.** Some botanists specialize in learning about trees, wood, or forests. Botanists can investigate tree diseases, study how trees live and grow, find out how forest animals depend on trees, or explore how trees are used by people.

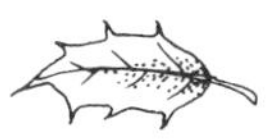

A botanist may work for a university, a paper manufacturer, a city museum, a government research project, or an environmental program. Some botanists make detailed drawings of trees and other plants, and some are lucky enough to explore jungles and rain forests.

Park rangers and **foresters** also study trees. All of these people have been trained and educated for their type of work.

Famous Families

Botanists who study trees have grouped them into **families.** In each family, there may be many types of trees. These different types are called **species.**

Here are some of the most common and well-known families of trees, with examples of species in each family.

From a high fire tower, a state forest ranger scans the landscape for plumes of smoke.

Pine Family

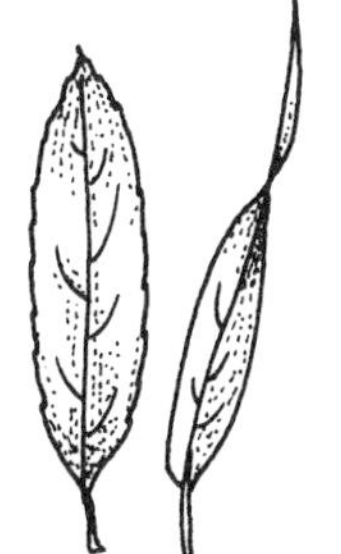
Willow Family

Elm Family

Walnut Family

Beech Family

Birch Family

Rose Family

Maple Family

Family	Species
Pine Family	Eastern White Pine, Douglas Fir, Black Spruce, Virginia Pine
Willow Family	Pacific Willow, Weeping Willow, Eastern Cottonwood, Quaking Aspen
Walnut Family	Black Walnut, Shagbark Hickory, Pecan
Birch Family	Paper Birch, Yellow Birch, Red Alder, Eastern Hophornbeam
Beech Family	American Beech, Northern Red Oak, White Oak, Blackjack Oak
Elm Family	American Elm, Slippery Elm, Hackberry
Rose Family	Common Apple, Black Cherry, American Plum
Maple Family	Sugar Maple, Red Maple, Silver Maple, Box Elder

There are about 1,000 species of tree in North America. Most grow wild and are native to North America. But many species have been introduced from other countries.

The Name Game

Names given to trees sometimes change. People living in one area may call a tree one name, but people living somewhere else identify the same tree by a different name. For example, the **eastern white pine** of North America is often planted in Great Britain. People there call it the **Weymouth pine.**

The **Pepperidge** is also called the black tupelo, black gum, horn pine, or sour gum.

A name for a tree that was used 100 years ago may not be used today. About the time of the Civil War, a common northern spruce was called the **double spruce.** Today, we call it the **black spruce.**

Here are some examples of different names used for the same species of tree.

One Person Calls It	Another Person Calls It
Tulip Tree	Yellow Poplar
Paper Birch	Canoe Birch or White Birch
Virginia Pine	Scrub Pine or Jersey Pine
Black Birch	Sweet Birch or Cherry Birch
Larch	Hackmatack or Tamarack
American Sycamore	Buttonwood or Planetree

Eastern white pine is native to the eastern U.S., but it is planted in other parts of the country, and even in England.

Here's Help

To stop the confusion about the names of trees, botanists have given scientific names to trees around the world. These names are made up from Latin and Greek words. Botanists from any country can use these scientific names, so they all know exactly what species someone is talking about.

At the back of this book (pp. 116–121), you'll find a list of the common names of trees, along with their scientific botanical names. The family that each tree belongs to is listed also.

Douglas Fir

"I think that I shall never see
A poem as lovely as a tree."

Alfred Joyce Kilmer
Trees (1913)

Record Setters

Some trees grow to an enormous height. The **redwoods** and **giant sequoia** trees of northwestern North America are famous for their huge size. Both species often grow more than 200 feet (60 m) tall. Some have even reached over 300 feet (90 m) high.

In the same area of the Pacific Northwest, several other types of trees grow to 200 feet or more.

Douglas Fir	Ponderosa Pine
Western Hemlock	Noble Fir
Sitka Spruce	Incense Cedar

But most trees never grow to such enormous heights. In fact, most common trees, even in a forest, grow to only about 50 to 80 feet (15 to 24 m) tall.

Growing Cycles

The life cycle of a huge forest tree may span hundreds or even thousands of years. Lots of human generations may pass in the time that a tiny seed sprouts, grows tall, and is finally killed by lightning, a forest fire, or by woodcutters. Many more years will pass before the dead tree completely decays or rots and returns nutrients to the forest soil.

What Makes a Tree Grown-Up?

Trees are usually considered **mature** when they first **bear flowers, fruit, or seeds**. An apple tree might blossom when it is less than ten years old. Hawthorn, shadbush, and other fruit or berry trees may bloom when they are young, also.

But many forest species, like oak or maple trees, may take many years before they produce seeds. After a tree has grown its first flowers, fruit, or seeds, it may continue to grow taller and taller. So it can be considered a mature tree when it flowers, but the tree might still not have reached its full size!

Timber workers and woodcutters consider a forest tree to be mature when it's big enough to cut for lumber. Some trees, like aspens, are cut down for making pulp or woodchips. And they can be cut while the trees are still relatively young.

Young seedlings of American longleaf pine don't look like trees at all—they just look like a big clump of grass!

Only a single species of tree is usually grown on a tree farm or plantation. But a natural forest consists of many different species growing together.

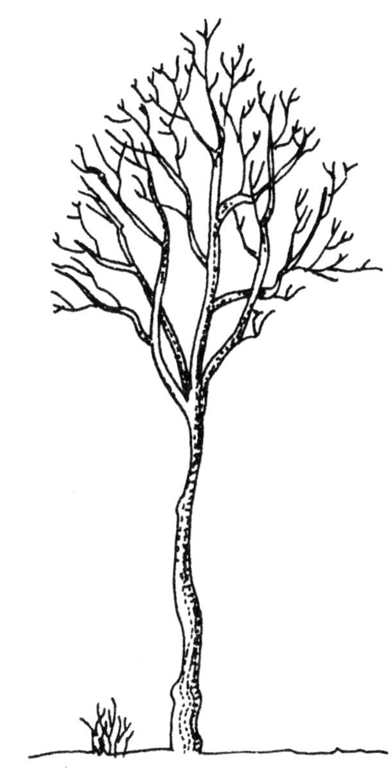

Bebb Willow in winter

Tall Tales

Climate and soil conditions may cause a tree to grow faster and larger in one area than a tree of the same species and age that's growing in a different location.

Trees and other plants always grow better when there is good soil and adequate water. We would never see forests of oak and maple growing successfully in the sandy dry soil of the desert. But the land surrounding lakes, rivers, and streams can support healthy tree growth.

If you live near the Great Lakes, you'll find plenty of forested land nearby. But if you live in open grasslands and dry plains, you may see very few trees.

The simple, fan-shaped leaves of ginkgo make it easy to identify.

Old-Timers

The oldest living trees on Earth are thousands of years old. In the United States, the oldest tree was a **bristlecone pine** that was 4,900 years old—but that tree was cut down with a chainsaw. The oldest tree now is another bristlecone, named Methuselah—it's about 4,600 years old. Other bristlecone pines in North America are judged to be well over 1,000 years old.

In the forests of the Pacific Northwest, many **Douglas fir** trees are over 200 years old. **Sitka spruce** and **western hemlock** in the same area may be that old, also. Some botanists and foresters think some of these trees may even be 500 or 600 years old. They would have been seedlings long before European settlers ever came to North America.

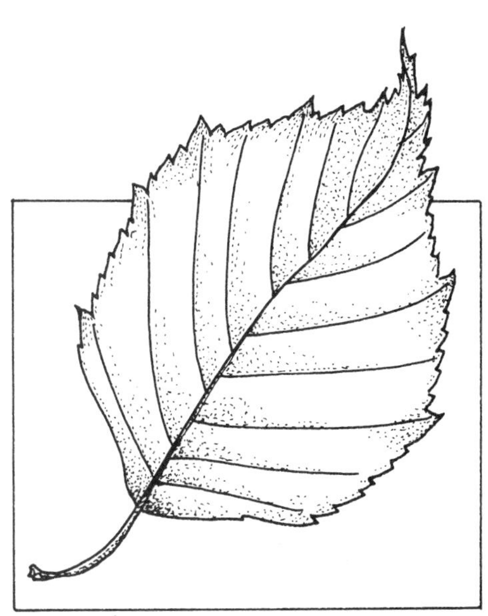

Birch trees have grown on Earth for millions of years.

In the Days of the Dinosaurs

Trees were growing on Earth long before human life developed. There were trees during the Cretaceous period, the time when dinosaurs like Triceratops and Lambeosaurus lived. We know this because **fossil** tree leaves have been found that are millions of years old. In the United States, fossil birch leaves have been found that are about 30 million years old.

Fossil leaves from trees in the **Willow, Maple,** and **Laurel families** have been found, too. Since these fossil leaves look so much like modern tree leaves today, scientists can tell which family they belong to.

A scientist who studies fossil tree leaves, fossil wood, and amber is called a paleobotanist.

It's the Same Old Thing

Some trees have hardly changed over millions of years. Fossil leaves of the **ginkgo** tree look almost exactly like the leaves of a ginkgo today. This unusual tree grew during the Triassic period—over 150 million years ago.

The ginkgo was thought to be extinct, since it was known only by its fossils. But a group of living ginkgoes was discovered in China, and now this tree is planted throughout North America in parks and along city streets.

The Pepperidge tree is known by several other names, including black tupelo and sour gum.

Hunks of Trunks

In Arizona's Petrified Forest National Park, huge fossilized tree trunks provide clues to what trees were like over 100 million years ago. These fossil trunks lie on the ground in big chunks and hunks, and others are whole logs. These fossils are so perfect that even the growth rings can be seen. The park protects these fossil trunks so that visitors can see them and scientists can study them.

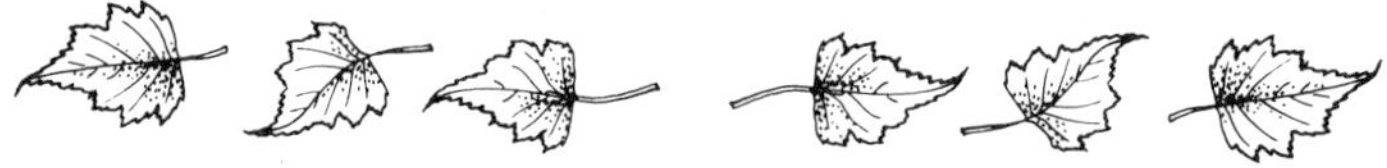

Hands Off!

Poison sumac usually grows as a small shrub, but sometimes it gets about 20 feet (6 m) tall—like a small tree. Each petiole has several leaflets with smooth edges on it. The middle vein of each leaflet is red or reddish. This field mark will help you to identify it. The bark of poison sumac is smooth and gray. Loose clusters of greenish flowers blossom in the summer, and these turn into pale, whitish berries.

Poison sumac likes to grow in wet areas, such as swamps and wet, boggy woods. This extremely poisonous tree grows in the East, from the Great Lakes area of Canada and the U.S., to all states along the Atlantic coast south to Florida, and west to Texas.

NEVER TOUCH the leaves, twigs, bark, berries, or flowers of this small tree—at *any* time of the year! Even the smoke from burning poison sumac leaves will cause poisoning. NEVER, EVER pick the leaves of this plant!

Like its close relative the **poison ivy plant**, poison sumac will cause a severe skin rash, with intense itching, burning, and swelling. The skin may even become infected. Poisoning can last for weeks, and it's much more severe than the reaction caused by the poison ivy plant.

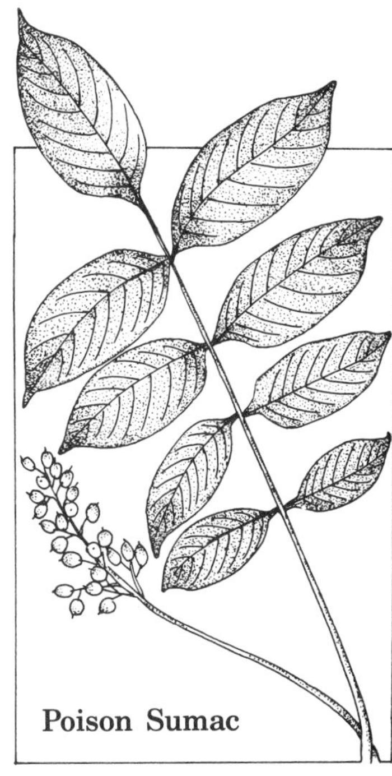

Poison Sumac

Other species of sumac are not poisonous at all. The **staghorn sumac**, which has fuzzy stems and fuzzy, red berries, is not poisonous. It usually grows in sunny, dry places. Another member of the **Sumac family** is the **cashew** tree, from which we get the unique, curved cashew nuts. And the **pistachio** is also a member of the Sumac family! Few people who eat cashew nuts or pistachio nuts realize that these delicious treats belong to the same family as the poison sumac.

Patches of snow in the background show that maple trees are tapped very early in the spring. These metal sap buckets are hanging on red maples.

— 2 —

Spring

Spring is a season of new growth and sprouting seeds. As temperatures climb, leaf buds and flowers open slowly to the sun.

Deciduous trees, like maple, oak, birch, and willow, grow a complete new set of leaves. **Evergreens**, like spruce and pine, add fresh new needles to their twigs.

Small acorns lying half-hidden in the dead leaves of the forest floor split open. And they soon send their first strong roots downward into the moist soil. Everything seems to be turning green and growing all at once!

Maple Sugar Time

Have you ever had pancakes or hot oatmeal with **maple syrup?** Or maple sugar candies? That delicious sweet syrup and candy is made from native **sugar maple** trees. Early in the spring, these trees are "tapped" for their sweet sap, which is made into syrup. Sugar maples in Vermont, Maine, New Hampshire, New York, Wisconsin, Michigan, and other northern states are tapped for their sap. Plenty of Canadian maples are tapped also.

Here's how it's done.

- First, a small hole is drilled about an inch deep into the trunk of a healthy, mature sugar maple. Usually, the tree is at least 30 to 40 years old. **Red maple** trees are often tapped for their sap, too.
- Then, a metal "tap," or **spile**, is hammered into the hole.
- Sap from the tree drips out through the spile.
- Metal or plastic buckets are hung on the sturdy spile to collect the liquid sap. Sometimes, plastic tubes are connected to the spiles instead of buckets. The buckets are usually covered.
- As the buckets fill up with sap, they are emptied into a main collection kettle, or vat, inside a **sugarhouse**—the "sugar shack."

The sugar shack may be a barn, an open shed, or a building constructed just for making maple syrup. This is what happens in the sugarhouse.

- The main collection kettle is finally filled with fresh sap from the buckets.
- All day long a hot fire blazes under the kettle or vat.
- The maple sap is boiled and boiled until it thickens into syrup. The longer the sap is boiled, the darker and sweeter the syrup gets.
- The syrup is graded by color and then poured into containers to be sold. It takes about 40 gallons of tree sap to make just *one* gallon of syrup!

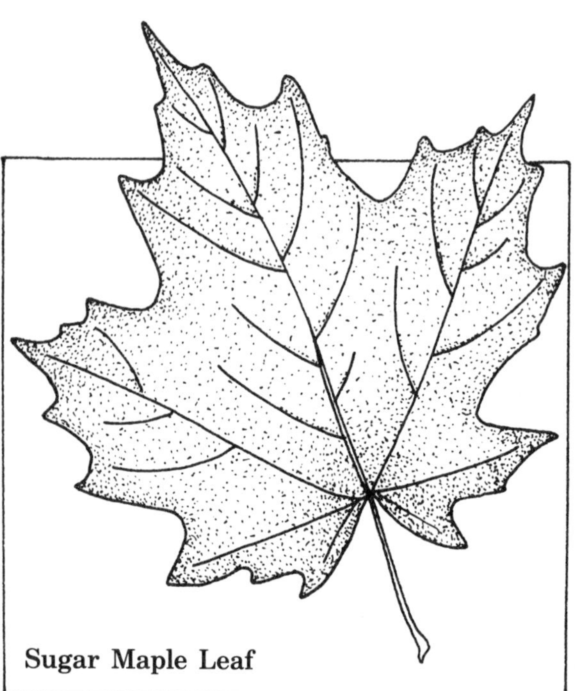

Sugar Maple Leaf

Maple syrup can be made very early in the spring—the end of February and during the month of March. Sometimes snow is still on the ground.

Visitors and workers at the sugar shack have a special treat by dripping the maple syrup right onto fresh snow for instant maple "ice cream."

You can also drizzle fresh maple syrup over crushed ice. In Vermont, workers eat this treat with sour pickles. The sugar is so sweet.

If the syrup is boiled even longer, it will turn solid after it's slowly cooled. That's how **maple sugar** is made. The thick, sweet sludge is poured into molds to make candy in the shape of stars, maple leaves, or log cabins. Hundreds of years ago, Native Americans collected maple sap, too, and they stored the hardened maple sugar in birch-bark boxes.

Sugar maples grow throughout the northeastern states and southeastern Canada, but only the trees in the colder regions are tapped. That's because the sweet sap flows best when mild spring days are followed by freezing nights.

Vermont, Maine, New York, Ohio, and Quebec produce most of the maple syrup made in North America. But **acid rain** and other **industrial pollution** may be a big danger for sugar maples. The health of these wonderful trees is already declining.

The white oak is the state tree of Connecticut, Illinois, and Maryland.

Big, Beautiful Blossoms

Flowering Trees

What are the biggest tree flowers? There are several species of trees from different regions that have large flowers.

Southern magnolia has huge, white, fragrant flowers with up to twelve petals, about 9 inches (22.5 cm) across. Other members of the **Magnolia family** have large white blossoms also—sweet bay, umbrella magnolia, and bigleaf magnolia. All are found in the southeastern United States, but some species of magnolia are grown in nurseries and planted near houses in more northern areas.

Flowering dogwood is a small tree native to the eastern states. But the tree is cultivated for its beautiful flowers outside its native range. Nursery-grown flowering dogwoods are planted along highways, in parks, and near buildings and schools.

The white petals are actually called **bracts** by botanists. They aren't really true petals, just a kind of specialized leaf that has coloring different from that of the true leaves. Each blossom of bracts is over 3 inches (7.5 cm) across. Some cultivated varieties of flowering dogwood also have pink bracts.

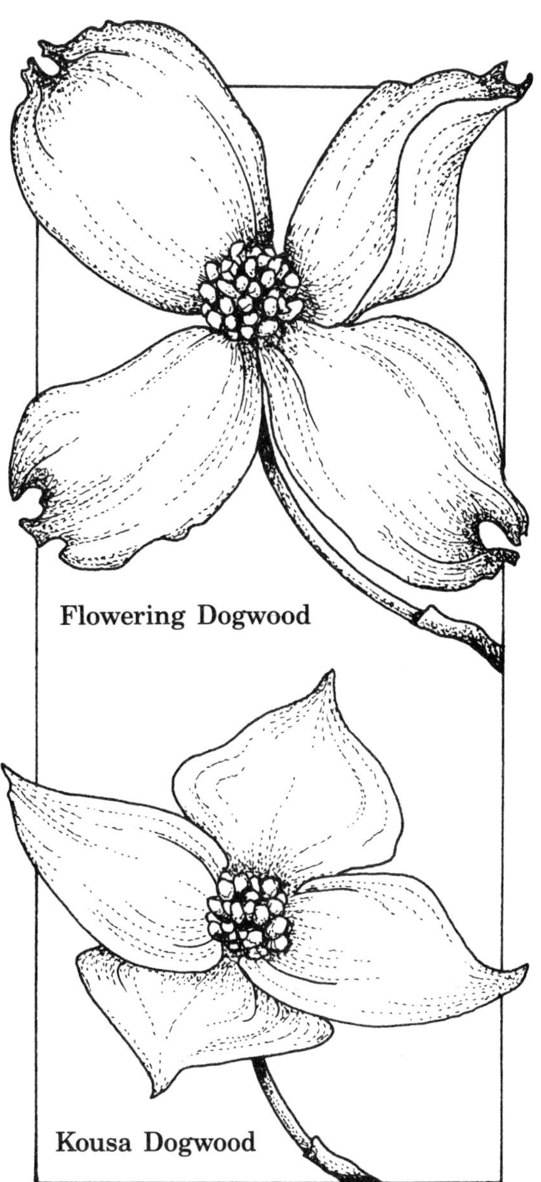

The big white "petals" are actually bracts, or modified leaves.

In the Pacific states and part of Pacific Canada, a very similar tree, the **Pacific dogwood**, has large white flowers also. **Kousa dogwood**, a species native to Japan, is grown in nurseries and planted for its blossoms also. Dogwoods in southern areas may bloom as early as March.

The large pink blossoms of a saucer magnolia open early in the spring.

Tulip tree, or yellow poplar, has big yellow green petals forming a tulip-like cup. The center of each "tulip" is orange. Each cup is about 2 inches (5 cm) across. The flowers begin to bloom very late in the spring, after the leaves have opened up. This tree is native to eastern states, but it is often planted beyond its natural range as a city street tree or a shade tree.

The Rose Family

It's easy to identify a rosebush—especially if you've ever been pricked by its thorns! But there are plenty of *trees* that belong to the same family as garden roses. Many of the trees in the **Rose family** have beautiful flowers.

The **common apple** is probably the most familiar tree in the Rose family. Hundreds of varieties of apples have been cultivated, but the flowers of these trees always look

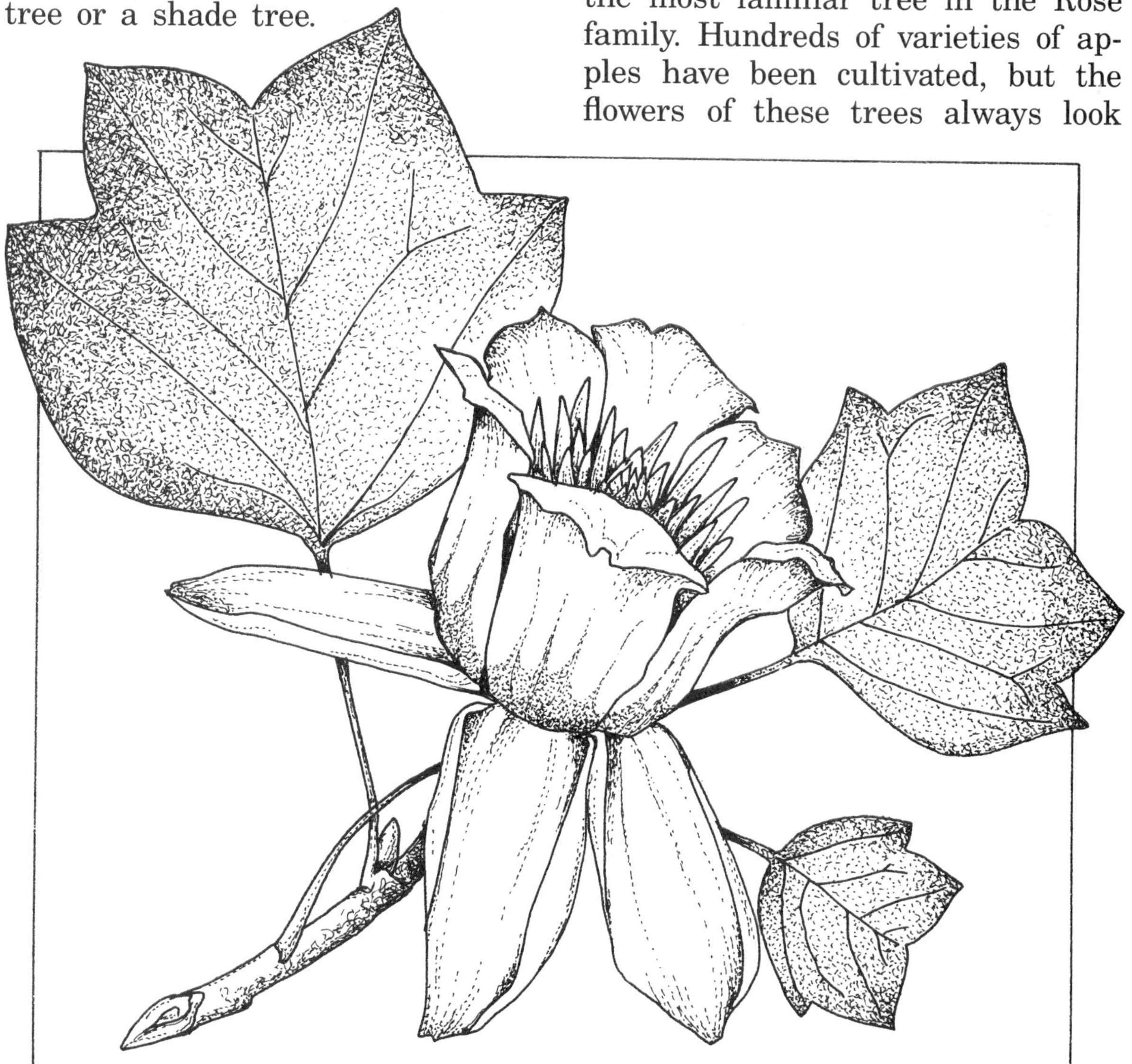

Tulip tree flowers are orange, yellow, and light green. They open very late in spring, after the leaves have opened.

pretty much the same. Each flower has five petals, which are pink or rose-colored.

Apple trees blossom in May, and a grove of these trees in full flower is a beautiful sight. The towns of Winchester, Virginia, and Arendtville, Pennsylvania, have apple blossom festivals in the spring to celebrate their flowering trees.

The delicate white flowers of serviceberry (shadbush) appear before the leaves are fully open.

Hawthorns are members of the Rose family also. There are over 100 species of wild, native hawthorns across North America. Most have leaves with teeth along the edge and twigs with long, sharp thorns. Each hawthorn flower has five petals, and depending on the species, the flowers are white, pink, dark rose, or white with red patterns.

Many hawthorns are kept small by pruning, but they can grow over 30 feet (9 m) tall. Hawthorns are often planted along shopping centers and near public buildings. The fruit of these trees is eaten by many species of bird in the fall. Cultivated varieties are available from nurseries.

Serviceberry is also called **shadbush** because its white flowers open at the beginning of the fishing season, when fish called *shad* are caught in rivers and streams. The flowers are white with five petals, and they bloom before the leaves of the trees have opened all the way. Serviceberry can grow as tall as 50 feet (15 m), but some related species are just small shrubs. They all have similar flowers. The different species of serviceberry trees and shrubs can be found across most of North America.

The flavoring in cola sodas is made from the seeds of kola trees, native to western Africa.

Clusters of pink apple blossoms are a welcome sign of spring across North America.

Common choke cherry blossoms. This tree, often a shrub, is native to most of southern Canada and the northern U.S.

Other trees in the Rose family include species that produce familiar fruit or nuts. **Crab apples, pears, plums**, and **peaches** are members of the Rose family. So are **almond** trees. California celebrates its cultivated groves of almond trees each spring with tours of the flowering almonds in the San Joaquin Valley.

Cherry Blossom Time

Pin cherry, common choke cherry, wild black cherry, and **Canadian** and **American plum** trees are members of the Rose family also. Their flowers all have five petals each. All are native to North America, and they have flowers which blossom around early May.

The sweet cherries you buy in a market or eat in cherry pies and tarts are cultivated cherries. They were developed by tree growers from the **wild cherry** of Europe and Asia. Grown in nurseries, these cultivated cherries are planted for their beautiful blossoms and luscious fruit.

Each year, cherry blossom festivals are held in San Francisco, at the Brooklyn Botanical Gardens in New York, and in Macon, Georgia. Washington, D.C., has a cherry blossom festival to celebrate the thousands of **Japanese cherry** trees given to the U.S. by Japan. Crowds of visitors tour Washington each year just to see these beautiful trees in full bloom.

In the U.S. alone, there are over 700 million acres of forested land.

Woodland Tree Flowers

In woodlands and along roadsides throughout most of the eastern half of the U.S. and southeastern Canada, **red maples** blossom early in the spring. Each red maple flower is small, but a single tree bears an abundance of flowers, so an entire tree looks like a haze of red orange.

The small twigs of red maples are red also. A whole hillside or roadside of these trees in full bloom is wonderful. They are a bright and welcome sign of spring.

Are you wearing a tree? Rayon cloth is made from chemically treated wood pulp!

Once the flowers fall, the ground is littered with the red orange blossoms. This gives you a good chance to look closely at them. Several flowers grow together in a cluster.

Other species of maple have similar flowers. **Sugar maple** and **Norway maple** both have greenish or yellowish flowers.

Decorative clusters of oak leaves are part of the design on some French and German coins.

Each Canada plum flower has five petals, which helps identify this tree as a member of the Rose family.

Red maple flowers. The flowers, twigs, and leaf buds are all reddish.

Catkins and Pussy Willows

The flowers of **black birch, paper birch, yellow birch**, and other species of birch trees are called **catkins**. You can see unopened catkins on birches during the winter, but in spring the catkins open up. They don't look very much like flowers, but they are. Each long, dangling catkin is actually made up of many tiny flowers. Birch catkins open up early in the spring, before the leaves have appeared.

The Willow family includes over 300 species worldwide.

Other kinds of trees have catkin flowers also. Trees in the Willow family, such as **quaking aspen, weeping willow**, and different species of **cottonwood** all have catkins. Many of them have a fuzzy, furry, or cottony appearance.

Pussy willow is well known for its silky, furry catkins. It usually grows as a shrub (less than 15 feet or 4.5 m tall), but sometimes grows much larger. Pussy willow grows wild across most of the northern U.S. and southern Canada, but it is also sold in markets or at garden centers.

Native Americans of the Cheyenne, Blackfoot, and Pawnee nations used the wood of osage orange trees to make hunting bows.

The flowers of the Bebb willow are known as catkins.

A chickadee inspects the catkins of a large-toothed aspen for insects.

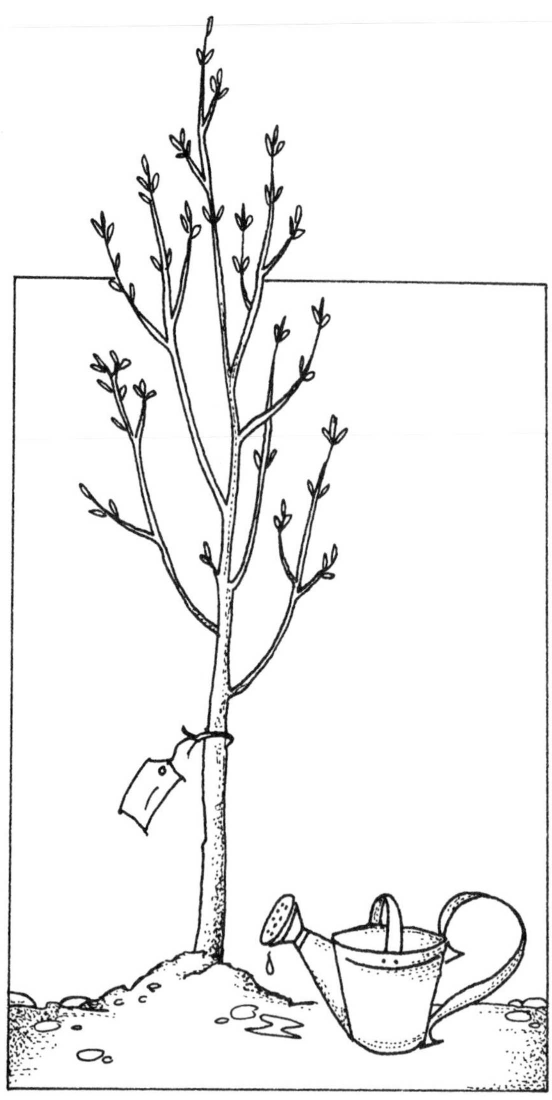

When you plant a young tree, leave its identification tag on, so you'll remember exactly what kind of tree it is.

Celebrate Spring!

Every spring, Americans celebrate **Arbor Day** by planting trees. Young tree saplings are planted near schools, office buildings, and along city streets. Arbor Day started in 1872 in Nebraska. While almost all other holidays seem to celebrate the past, Arbor Day is one that truly recognizes the future. Trees can live for hundreds, even thousands, of years!

National Arbor Day is honored on the last Friday in April in the U.S., but state Arbor Days may occur in February or May.

Since it's warmer in the southern states, you can plant a young sapling very early in the year—Arbor Day is observed in February in Georgia and Mississippi. Up north in Maine or in North Dakota, Arbor Day trees are planted in May, after all threats of a frost pass.

In Spain, trees are celebrated during the Fiesta del Arbol, held in late March.

Plant a Tree

You may have a chance to participate in an Arbor Day celebration at your school, or you and your family may decide to plant a tree near your house for a special family occasion, or to celebrate Earth Day or May Day. Here are a few planting pointers.

 Choose a healthy-looking sapling. The buds should not yet be open, and they shouldn't look dried out. The bark should not be scraped or damaged.

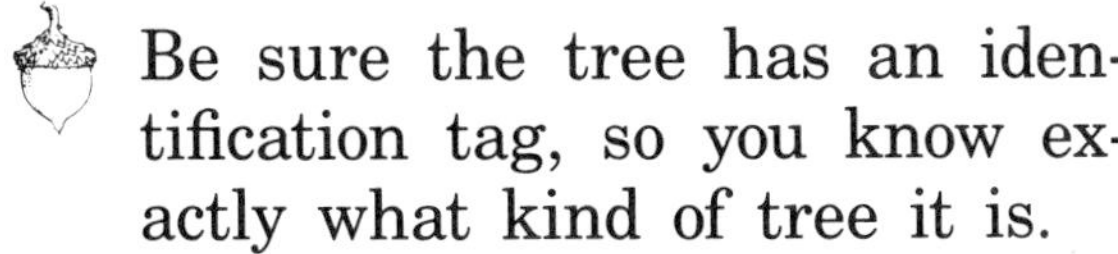
Be sure the tree has an identification tag, so you know exactly what kind of tree it is.

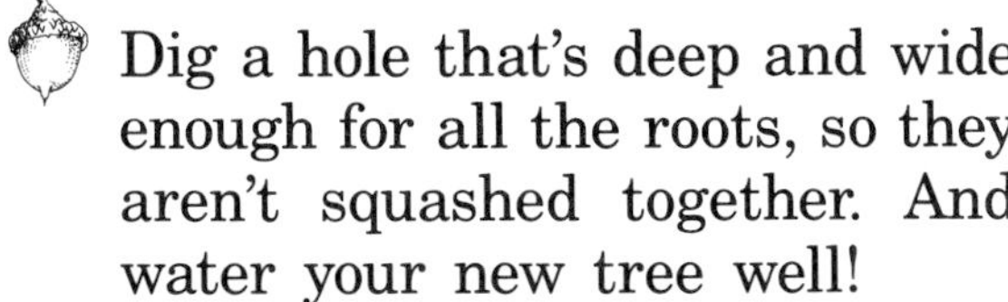
Dig a hole that's deep and wide enough for all the roots, so they aren't squashed together. And water your new tree well!

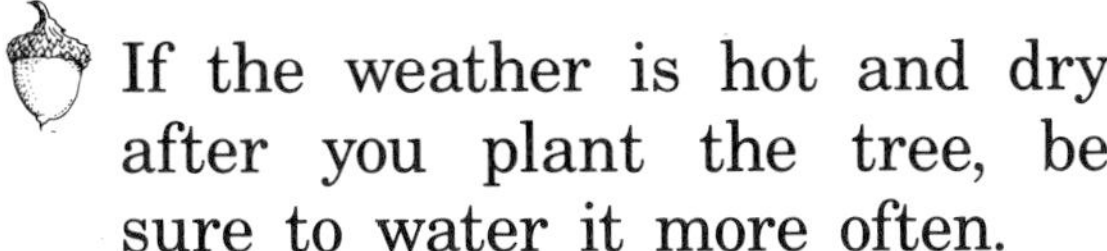
If the weather is hot and dry after you plant the tree, be sure to water it more often.

Many people plant trees on their birthdays. That way, they can watch how the tree has grown each year, as they grow older themselves. You can watch your own new tree grow taller year after year. You'll see how it changes with the seasons and observe how the bark thickens.

You may want to plant a tree that will have flowers. Hawthorn, crab apple, and flowering dogwood are available at many nurseries and garden centers. In the southern states, **eastern redbud** is a popular tree with beautiful rose pink flowers and heart-shaped leaves. Let the workers at the nursery help you choose a tree that will do well in your particular neighborhood.

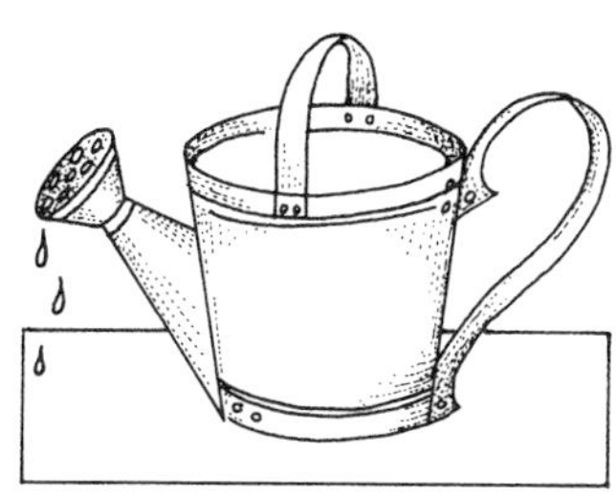
Don't forget to water your tree when the weather is dry!

The new spring growth on a balsam fir. The leaves are folded closely together, but as they grow, each needle will curve outward like those lower down.

The Evergreen Advantage

Evergreen trees are popular to plant in the spring also. Since they have green leaves all year long, they will be attractive even in the middle of winter. Evergreens can be planted near buildings or in rows to make a hedge. Most can be trimmed and pruned to keep a rounded shape or a "Christmas tree" shape.

Here are some evergreens that are often sold in nurseries, on tree farms, or by state and province forestry agencies—**American arborvitae** (northern white cedar), **Scotch pine, eastern hemlock, balsam fir**, and **blue spruce**.

When you decide what kind of tree you want to plant, leave the identification tag on it. The tag will help you remember what kind of tree you have. That's a big help if other trees are nearby!

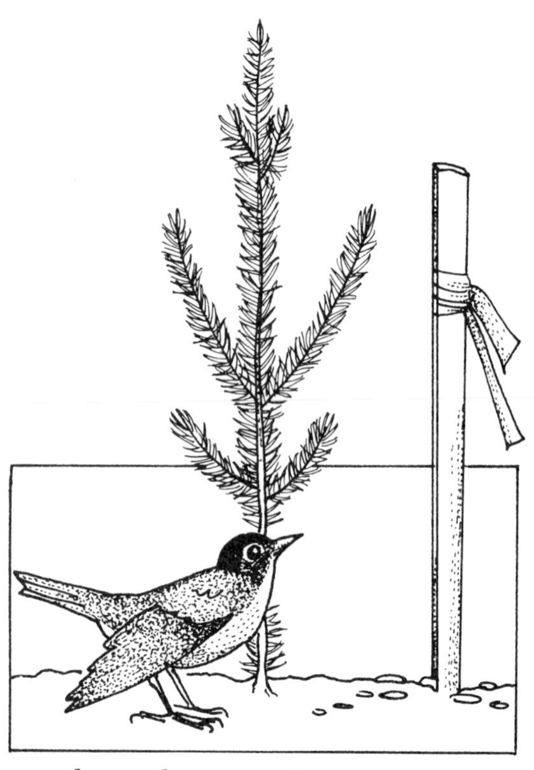

A wooden stake set in the ground near your seedling will help mark its place.

Starting Small

Small tree **seedlings** may be offered for planting early in the spring in your area. Scout troops, nurseries, and forestry offices sometimes offer seedlings for free or for low prices. Because they are so small—a foot (.3 m) tall or less—tree seedlings should have a wooden stake or marker placed nearby. That way, you can find them easily. If a small seedling isn't marked in this way, you might step on it accidentally!

A seedling balsam fir is a good choice of evergreen, and it's easy to plant.

Seedlings of evergreen trees, like **pines** or **spruces**, are often sold in large numbers. Measure your new seedling to see how tall it is, and write its height on your calendar. Then you can measure it again in the fall to see how much it has grown.

Starting a Tree from Cuttings

You can grow a new tree right from the cut branches or twigs of a much older, larger tree. **Willow trees** are the easiest to grow from cuttings. **Weeping willow, black willow, Bebb willow**, or **Pacific willow** are all good species to try. Here's how to do it.

- Cut off a small, healthy branch that's about a foot or two long and that has plenty of buds on it.
- Put the branch, or cutting, in a bottle of water so that less than half of it is submerged. Always be sure you keep water in the jar to cover any delicate new roots.
- In a few weeks, watch for roots starting to grow into the water. After several weeks, the whole inside of the bottle may be crowded with roots!
- When there are plenty of roots growing, then you can plant your new willow cutting outdoors. Mark its location with a stake or brightly colored tag, so you won't forget to water it in dry weather.

Other members of the **Willow family**, like the **trembling aspen**, can be grown from cuttings also, although they are a little more difficult. Cuttings are an easy way to create several trees from just one tree. They're also a great way to begin a new tree if a big willow has been cut down or blown down in a storm. Just snip off some twigs, and start growing your new willows!

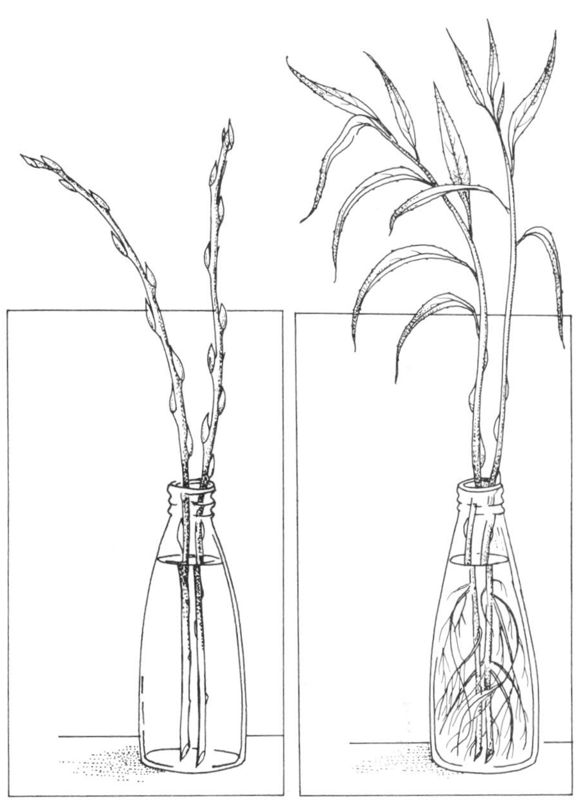

Set a willow cutting in a jar of water, and start growing a tree! In a few weeks, your willow cutting will develop roots and leaves.

If you start lots of cuttings, you can grow your own "miniature indoor forest." Aspens and willows work best. Then, when the little trees are ready, you can plant them outside.

Look for New Growth

By the end of spring, you can find plenty of evidence of new growth on trees. Look for fresh spring growth at the ends of twigs and branches, where the leaf buds have opened up.

How long does it take for a leaf to open up completely? It is different for different trees, and the weather has a part to play, too. A very dry winter and spring may delay the opening of tree leaves.

Look for fresh spring growth on evergreens such as pine, spruce, hemlock, or fir. The new leaves on these trees are usually soft and bright green compared to older leaves.

Find a small tree or a tree with low branches, so that you can inspect the opening of the new leaves easily. You'll be able to see the leaf buds on the twigs get bigger, opening slowly over a few days (or several days, depending on the weather). The leaves will finally start spreading out, until they are completely flat and open.

Look for evergreen "candles"! The new spring growth on pines often looks like candles on a Christmas tree. The new, light green tips grow straight upward from the branch like thin candles.

These new spring leaves may seem fragile, thin, and delicate. But they'll remain on the branches through months of blazing sun, or high heat and drought, and storms, winds, and hungry insects. Leaves are paper thin, but they can survive some tough environmental conditions!

— 3 —

Summer

If summer months are really hot where you live, you'll enjoy the shade of a big tree. This is the time of year when all the leaves are fully opened and most flowering trees have already bloomed. Seeds, nuts, fruits, and berries are developing now and will ripen by autumn. Summer rains and mild temperatures combine to keep trees healthy and growing.

But remember—it may be summer where *you* live, but it's winter in another part of the world! If you live in Sydney, Australia, summertime lasts from December to February. But that's winter up in Toronto, Canada!

Battle against Bugs

In the summer, not only do you see lots of leaves and green, growing things, but you'll see lots of insects, too.

Every summer, trees growing in forests and cities alike may suffer damage from insects. Here are some of the problems insects can cause.

Wood-boring beetles munch into bark or branches, damaging the sapwood.

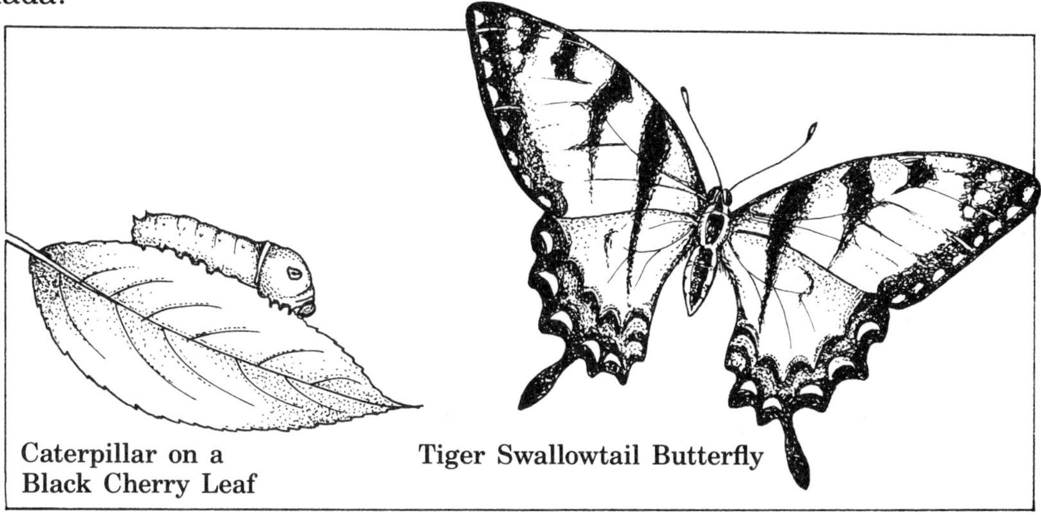

This smooth, bright green caterpillar (left) will develop into the beautiful tiger swallowtail butterfly (right). The caterpillar feeds on black cherry leaves but does little harm at all.

The hairy caterpillar of a Gypsy moth feeds voraciously on oak leaves, pine needles, and aspen leaves.

Caterpillars or **moths** devour leaves—sometimes until the trees are bare. **Tent caterpillars, hemlock loopers**, and **Gypsy moth caterpillars** are some of these harmful insects.

The **larvae** (young) of **sawflies** eat the needles of evergreen trees. These trees may die if all their needles are eaten.

Leaf miners are very tiny. They burrow through the leaves of birch trees and holly, leaving just a "skeleton" of the leaf.

Defoliation

When one kind of insect appears in great numbers in a forest, or even on a single tree, that's called an **infestation**. An apple tree infested with tent caterpillars may lose all its leaves in just a few weeks, as the caterpillars eat them up.

A whole forest of oak and pine trees can have its leaves devoured by an infestation of **Gypsy moth caterpillars**. These fuzzy caterpillars eat and eat until the forest looks like winter again—all the leaves are gone!

When a tree has lost all its leaves to insects or to a disease it has been **defoliated**. Defoliation can kill some trees. But if it just happens once, the tree may survive and grow new leaves when the infestation of insects has passed. Trees defoliated two summers in a row may not survive.

Caterpillars of Chinese silk moths feed on the leaves of mulberry trees.

Caterpillars to Watch For

Not all caterpillars are harmful to trees. A healthy young black cherry tree can feed the caterpillars of the **tiger swallowtail butterfly**. These caterpillars don't usually eat enough leaves to harm the tree, and they will turn into beautiful butterflies later in the year. The caterpillars are smooth, not fuzzy, and feed on **black cherry, willows,** and **tulip trees**. The caterpillars of the tiger swallowtail can be found across most of the U.S. and Canada.

Scouting for Trees

City Street Trees

If you live in a big city, you can still find trees near your school or apartment, in a local park, or right along the streets. Trees make city streets look more attractive. Rows of trees create a **windbreak**, slowing down gusts of wind. Trees even help to **reduce** the **noise** of traffic. They also provide cool shade when streets and paved lots get really hot in the summer sun.

Here are some species of tree often planted in cities and towns as **"shade trees"**—Norway maple, linden, silver maple, pin oak, box elder, and red maple.

Town Trees from Far Away

Many trees planted and grown in North American towns are not **native** to the area. They grow naturally **wild** in other areas or in other countries. These non-native species are cultivated in **nurseries** and **tree farms** across the U.S. and Canada, and they have **adapted** well to their new surroundings.

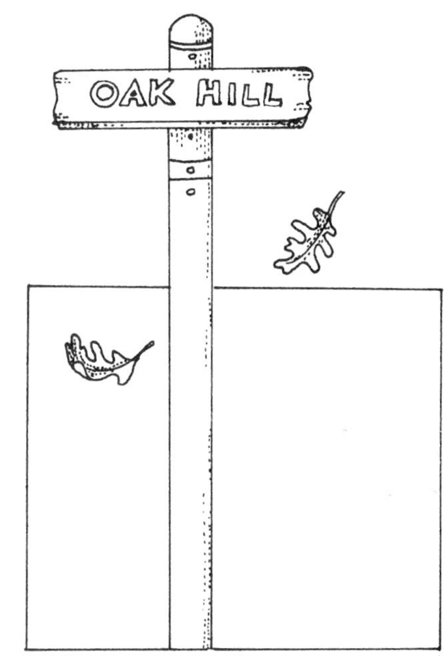

How many streets in your town are named after trees?

The **northern catalpa** is native to a small area in the central U.S., but it is planted successfully far north of its normal range. Catalpa trees have big, heart-shaped leaves and long, string-bean-like pods, so they are easy to identify. They also have large, fragrant flowers.

The silver maple is often planted along city streets and near buildings.

Horse chestnut trees are native to Asia and Europe, but they have been planted widely in North America. This tree is sometimes planted near a post office, city hall, or other public building. Horse chestnuts are members of the **Buckeye family**, as is the **Ohio buckeye**, the native state tree of Ohio.

The **ailanthus** tree, grown in New York City and other large cities and towns, is also called **"tree of heaven**." It is easily identified by its unusual seeds, which are winged, with a twist at the end, and a single seed in the middle.

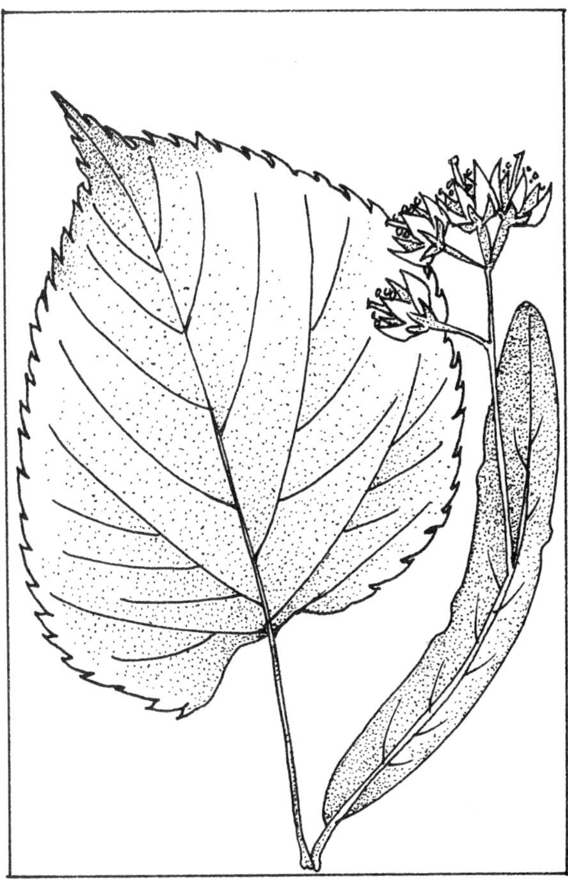

The American linden is also known as basswood. The flower clusters are attached to a leaf-like structure.

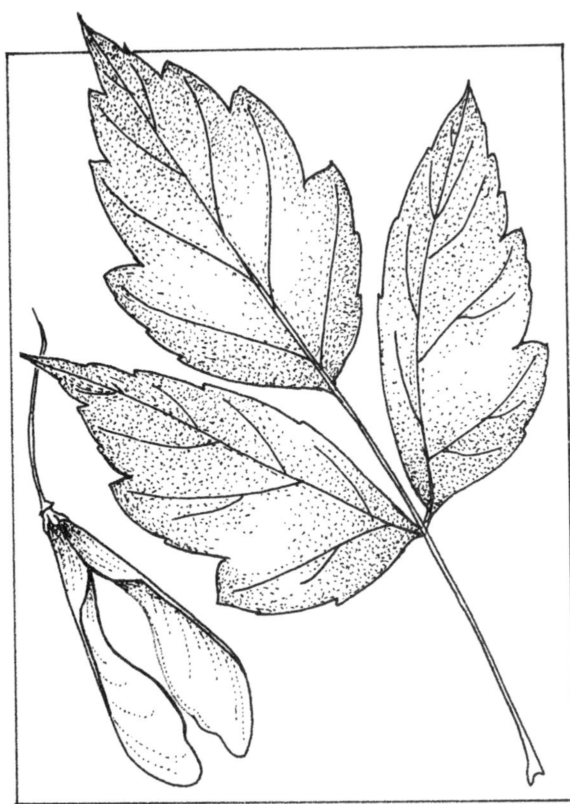

Box elder is a type of maple. The winged seeds are called samaras.

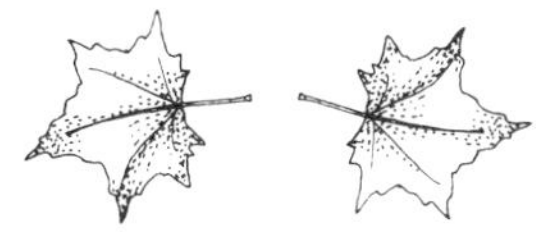

Norway maple, a common shade tree, is actually native to Europe and Scandinavia. It has been planted in North America for over 100 years. The leaves of the Norway maple are larger and wider than either the native sugar maple or red maple.

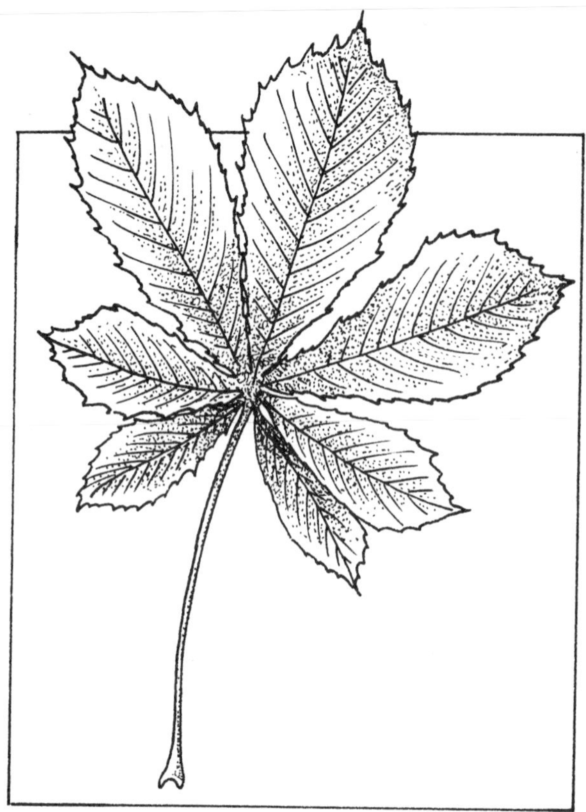

A horse chestnut leaf is divided into several leaflets, and all are attached to a single petiole, or stem.

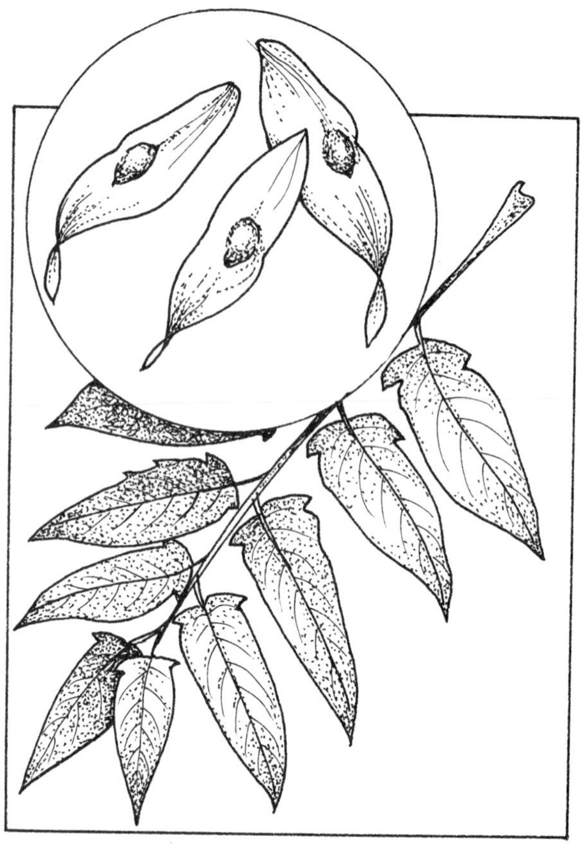

The ailanthus is native to southern China but often planted in North American cities. Each unusual winged seed has a twist.

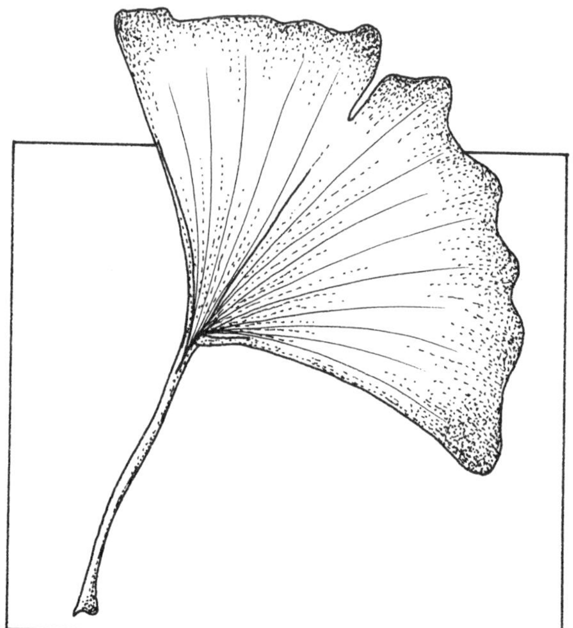

Ginkgo trees have unique, fan-shaped leaves.

Perhaps the most unusual city tree is the **ginkgo**, a native of China. The shape of its leaves has remained basically unchanged for millions of years. Fossilized ginkgo leaves show the same fan shape that the leaf has today.

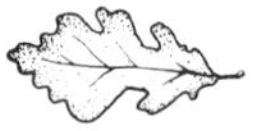

"A tree that may in summer wear
A nest of robins in her hair."

Alfred Joyce Kilmer
Trees (1913)

A Walk in the Park

Summer is the perfect time to look at trees in a **city park, botanical garden**, or **state** or **provincial park**. A **nursery, tree farm**, or an **arboretum** is a good place to visit, too.

Hiking trails are often named for the trees that grow along the paths.

An arboretum is a protected **sanctuary** where many different species of tree are grown. These trees are usually labelled with their species name. **Nature centers** and **science museums** often have **hiking trails** with labelled trees also.

These places make it easy to learn to identify trees that grow near you. You may also see some trees that come from far away. Museums allow you to see drawings and fossils of trees that grew long ago.

Trip Tips

Whether you visit a park, arboretum, or **national forest**, you're sure to find tree species you've never seen before. Look for differences in the texture of bark. Also look for different shapes and sizes of leaves, and compare the height of several species of tree.

Be sure to dress comfortably, and be prepared to walk around a lot. Take along a **notebook**, or even a **sketchbook**, so that you can draw pictures of the new leaves you find. If you have a **camera**, you'll want to get shots of flowering trees or trees that are really tall. Many parks and museums have **printed guides** that show pictures of the trees growing on the trails, along with their identification and interesting notes.

You'll also want to keep a special **tree watcher's notebook** of your own.

Identifying Summer Leaves

If you're on vacation from school, you'll have plenty of time to explore the leaves on trees in your neighborhood. Or you may go visiting or travelling during the summer, where you'll see new species of trees. Use the pictures on the next few pages to identify leaves from trees you've seen. The unusual shape of some leaves—like those of the **sweet gum** or the **tulip tree**—make them easy to match up with the pictures.

Once you've identified a few common trees, you'll find it easier to learn the names of others.

Leaf Identification

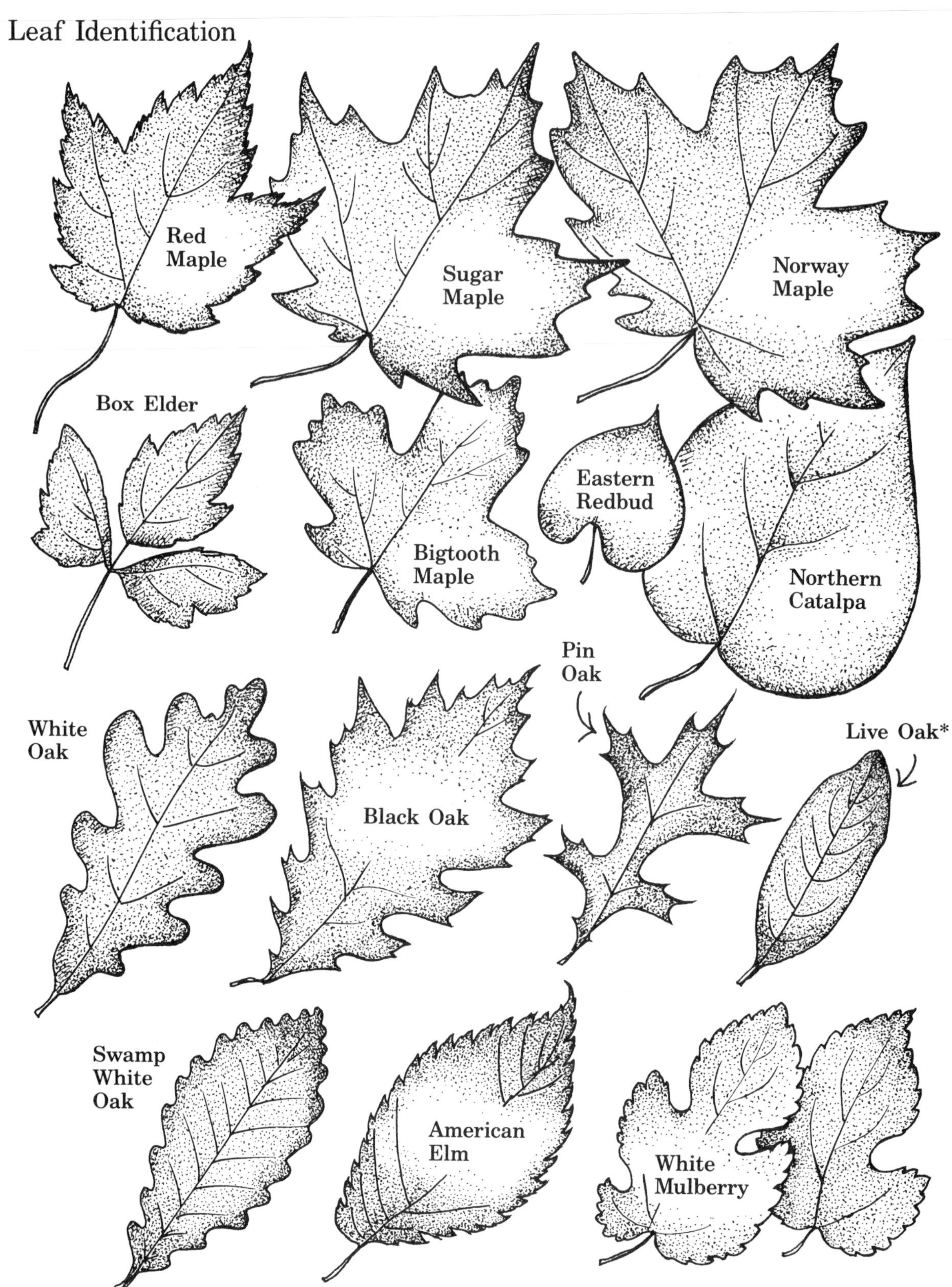

**Live oak is the only evergreen on this page.*

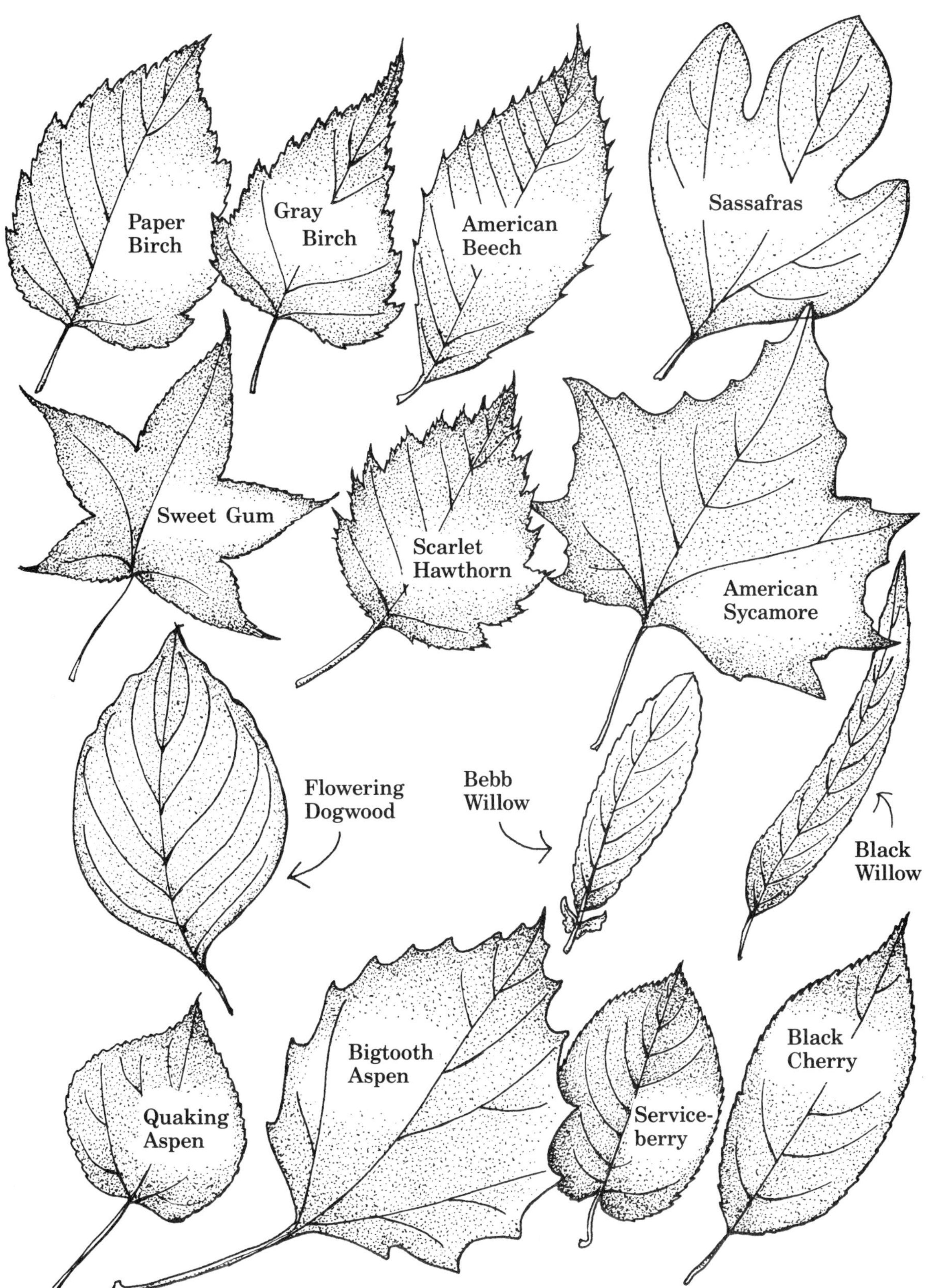
Paper
Birch
Gray
Birch
American
Beech
Sassafras
Sweet Gum
Scarlet
Hawthorn
American
Sycamore
Flowering
Dogwood
Bebb
Willow
Black
Willow
Bigtooth
Aspen
Quaking
Aspen
Service-
berry
Black
Cherry

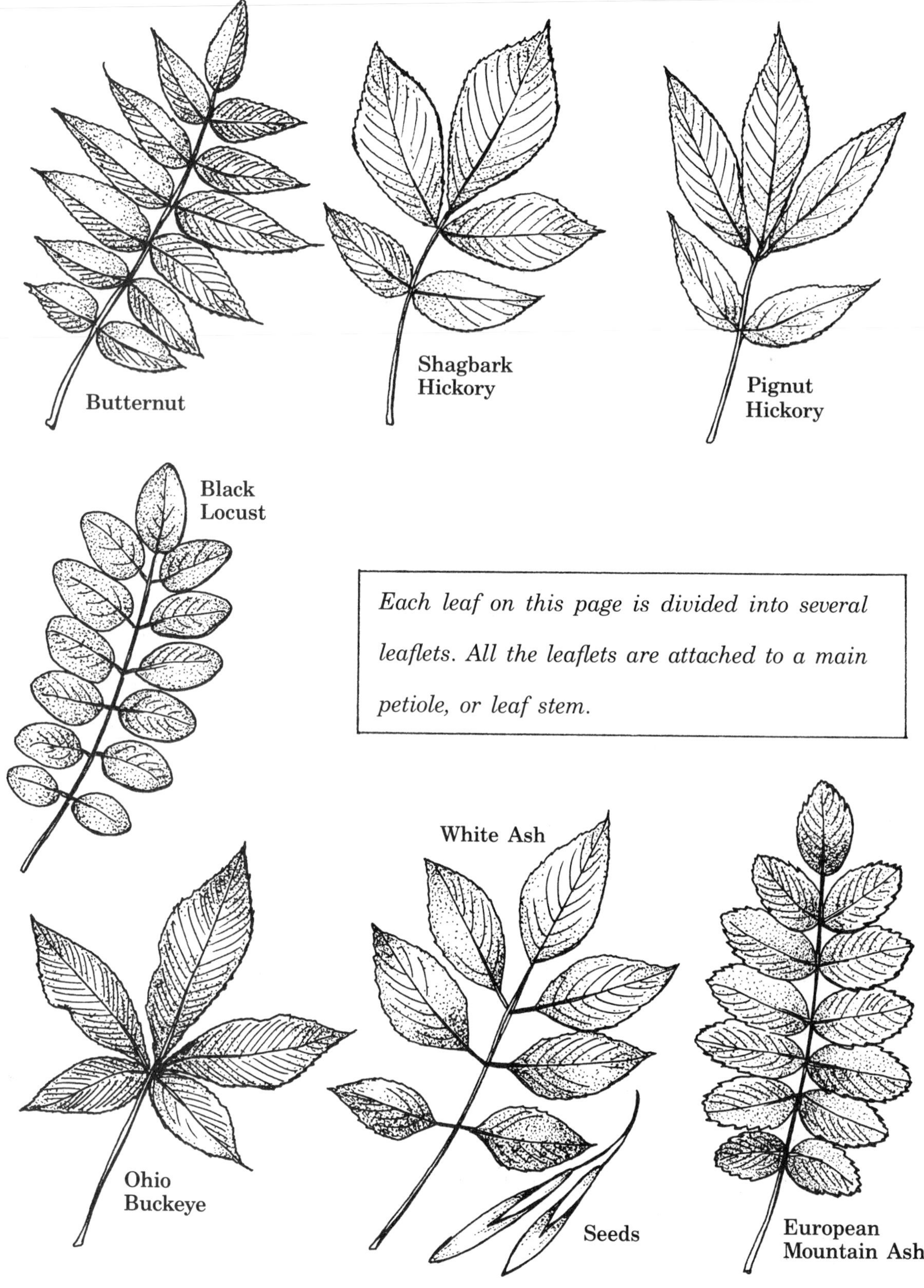

Each leaf on this page is divided into several leaflets. All the leaflets are attached to a main petiole, or leaf stem.

A leaf identification card is a great way to protect and preserve your pressed leaf.

Making Leaf Identification Cards

Tree leaves can be pressed flat and dried, and they'll last for years and years. A collection of pressed leaves mounted on **leaf identification cards** will give you an excellent record of the trees growing in your neighborhood. Here's how to get started.

Collect only a few leaves from trees around your home or school.

Choose leaves that have no insect damage.

Be sure to keep the petiole (leaf stem) attached.

Pressing the leaves flat is easy. Here's what you do.

Place your leaves between sheets of newspaper in layers.

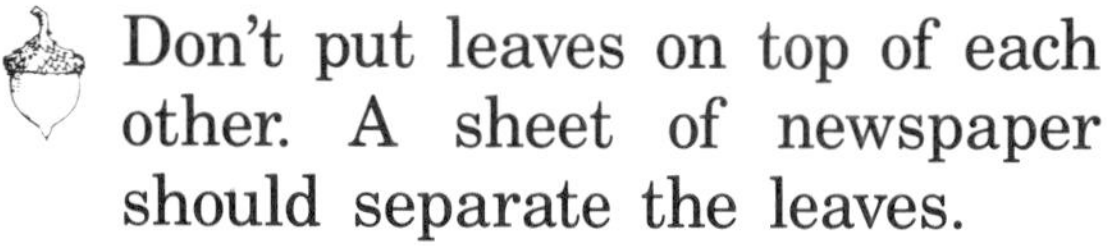
Don't put leaves on top of each other. A sheet of newspaper should separate the leaves.

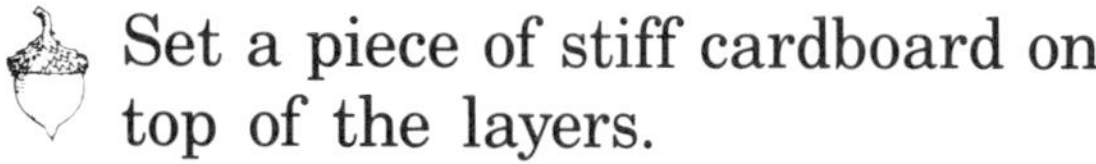
Set a piece of stiff cardboard on top of the layers.

Put some heavy books, or a big rock, on top of the cardboard. The weight will press the leaves flat, and the newspapers will absorb the moisture from the leaves so that they dry out.

If the weather is dry, your leaves will only need a week or so to dry out. If it's raining, or your house is damp, it will take a few more days.

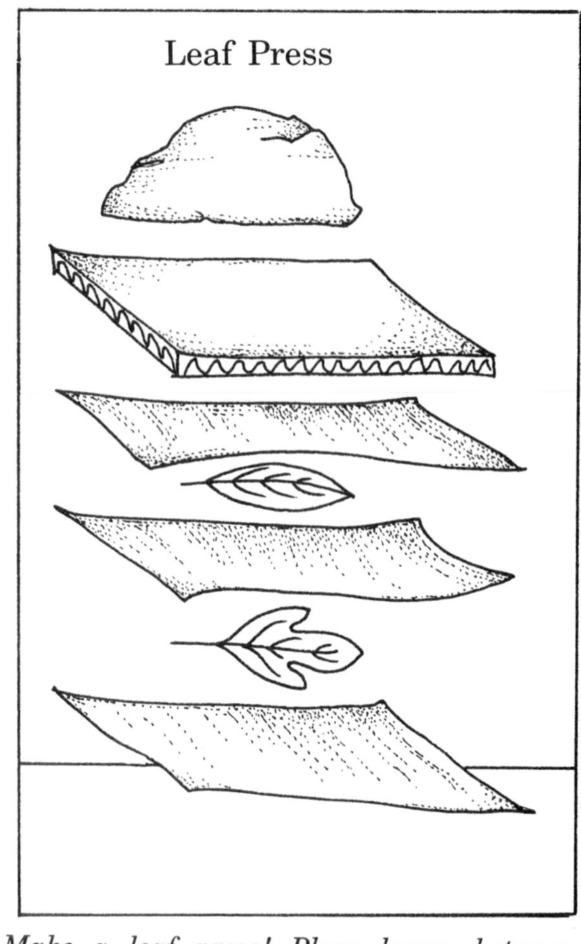

Make a leaf press! Place leaves between layers of newspaper and top them with stiff cardboard. Weight down the leaves with a rock or heavy book to press them flat.

Putting the Card Together

After you press the leaves, you can make a leaf identification card for each one. The cards will last for years. Here's how to put the card together.

Cut a piece of white paper into a rectangle or a square about 6 inches on each side. Then, cut a piece of stiff cardboard to match.

Use clear tape, or a dab of white liquid glue, to attach your leaf to the white paper. Glue or tape the white paper to the cardboard.

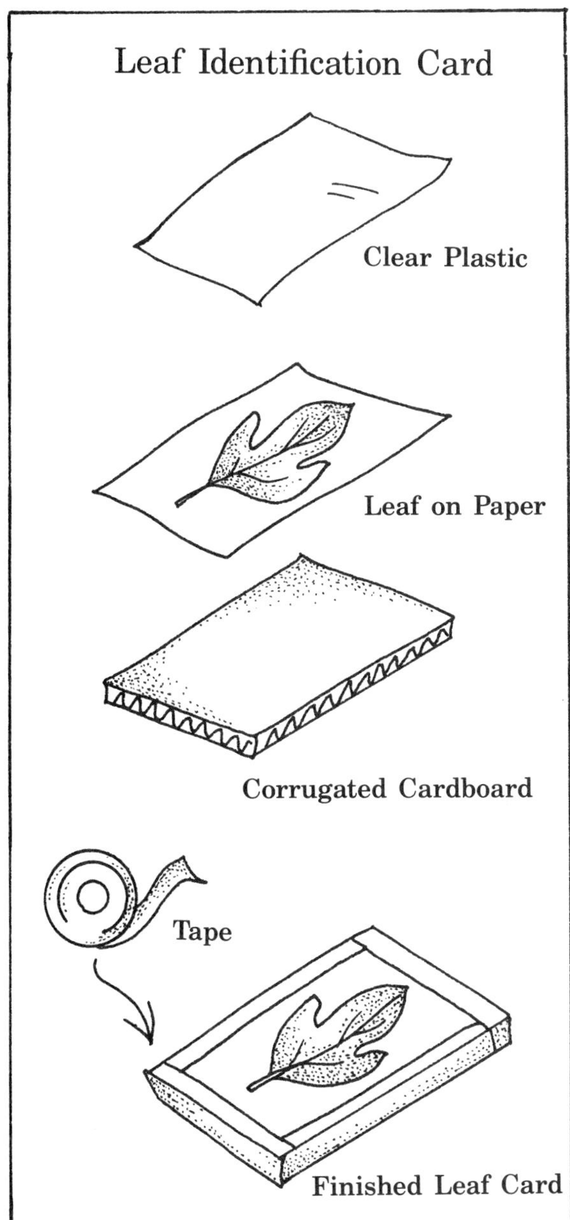

Make a leaf identification card. *Glue or tape a pressed leaf to white paper. Cover it with clear plastic, and place it on a backing of cardboard. Tape all the sides together.*

Cut a piece of clear plastic or acetate (saved from an old notebook page protector or from plastic packaging). Set this on top of the leaf.

Tape all four edges of the display together. Use colored tape for a more attractive card.

Now for the identification! On the back of the card, make four lines with a ruler. On the first line write the name of the tree. On the next lines write where the tree grows, the date the leaf was collected, and the name of the collector—you! It should look like this.

On the back of your leaf identification card, write the name of the tree, and where and when you found your specimen.

Maple samaras spin as they fall from the branches, like little helicopters.

If you trade leaf cards with a friend, you might be able to get cards of leaves you've never seen before. Take your leaf identification cards with you on a hike or on vacation. That way, you'll be able to compare them with the leaves on trees wherever you go.

Some trees in the Willow family have seeds with silky filaments that drift in the wind like tiny parachutes.

Also, use the **summer leaf guide** in this chapter to help identify the leaves of trees in your neighborhood. You can also match leaves with those of labelled trees at an arboretum or nature center. Teachers, parents, and friends may be able to help identify trees, too.

Making Leaf Prints

Using freshly collected leaves, you can make some artistic prints of leaves from trees in your neighborhood. Here's what you need to get started.

A few leaves with interesting shapes and veins. Oak and maple leaves are good, but the smooth leaves of black cherry don't work well.

Nontoxic paint or ink. Try finger paint or acrylic paint. Use dark colors like black, dark green, brown, or blue. The paint should be a little sticky instead of runny. Ink from a bottle is too runny, but an inked stamp pad works.

White paper or brown wrapping paper to print on. Paper cut from brown grocery bags is fine.

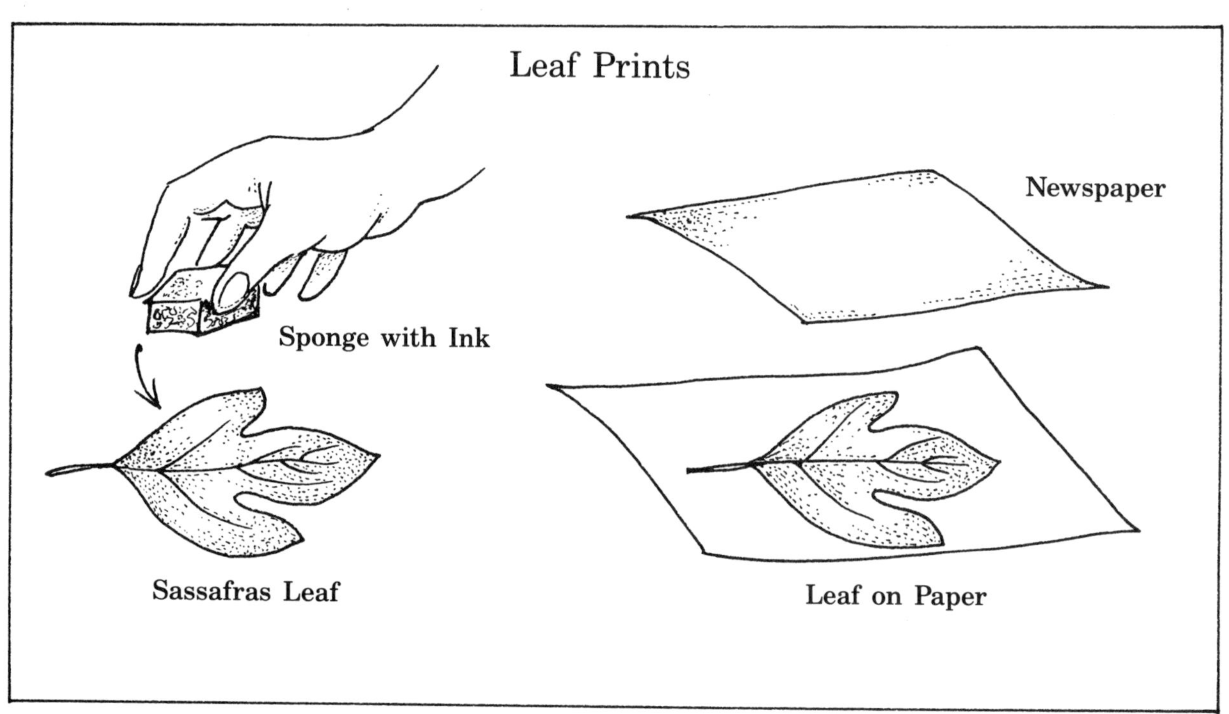

Here's how to make a leaf print.

Dab the paint or ink on the *underside* of the leaf. Use a piece of sponge or a damp, folded paper towel to dab the paint on. Put paint or ink on all parts of the leaf—even the petiole.

Carefully place the leaf with the painted side down on your paper. Cover the leaf with a sheet of newspaper, and press down *lightly*, making sure the edges of the leaf are pressed down onto the paper also.

Remove the newspaper and peel off the leaf.

The printed design will look like the real leaf pattern. You'll even be able to see the veins.

The same leaf can be used to make several prints, if you add more paint or ink to it. You'll need to experiment to find the right amount of paint. Too much paint will make dark blobs on the paper, but too little will prevent the veins or edges from printing.

Show Off Your Leaf Prints

Here are some creative ways to use your leaf prints.

Make several leaf prints on the same piece of paper, and then use it to wrap a gift. Or you could cover a schoolbook.

Use leaf-printed paper to cover the outside of an empty soup can, and use it as a pencil holder.

Decorate your writing paper or notebook paper with leaf prints when you send a letter to a friend. You'll be able to show them the kinds of trees that grow in your area. And maybe they'll send you a leaf print back!

Red Maple Leaf Print

Collector's Notes

Whether you collect a few leaves to make prints or to press and construct identification cards, remember: *Never damage the tree itself.* Remove only a few leaves. Look for trees that look healthy and have plenty of leaves. Be sure to ask for permission if the tree isn't on your own property.

Black Oak Leaf Print

Looking at Trees from around the World

If you're sitting indoors watching television, you can still find some new trees. Just watch the world news! Whenever the news reporter is talking outdoors, look at the background landscape closely.

Look for **palm trees** in the background when a reporter is talking from the Mideast. When news from Russia or Ukraine is being reported, look for the white trunks of **birch trees** in the distance. Watch for the many kinds of **pines** from around the world—Japan, Australia, Europe, and Scandinavia. You'll probably miss whatever the reporter is saying, but you'll be observing living trees from distant countries.

Sometimes trees *are* the news. During the summer, there may be reports about **forest fires**. Trees which provide **medicine**, such as the **Pacific yew**, have been in television news recently. **Fruit trees**, like orange or apple trees, make the news if they become threatened by **insect infestations** or bad weather.

Newspapers and magazines print articles about trees and forests. There are probably enough stories and pictures to start a **tree scrapbook** or even to make a **science fair project**.

The California fan palm, also called the Washingtonia palm, is native to southern California.

Palm Trees for the Sunny South

If you live in Canada or the northern U.S., your streets and parks won't be shaded with **palm trees.** But if you live in Hawaii, southern California, Florida, or other southern states, you'll see plenty of trees in the **Palm family**.

The trunks of palms rise up without dividing into branches. Most palms have leaves that grow from the very top of the trunk, like a cluster of graceful feathers. Some palm leaves look like huge fern leaves, while others spread out like a fan. Palm trees have green leaves throughout the year.

One of the most well-known members of this family is the **coconut palm**, which may grow to a height of 100 feet (30 m). The huge seeds of the coconut are sold in supermarkets across North America. Fresh coconut from the inside of the hull is a real treat for most people. So is the sweet liquid called **coconut milk** that you can drain from the coconut's center.

Most members of the Palm family grow in **tropical climates**, where the weather is like summer most of the time. In North America, there are about a dozen species of palm tree. Most are native to other countries, but they have adapted well to the southern and southwestern U.S. The **cabbage palm** of Florida and the Southeast is also called the **sabal palmetto palm**—it's the state tree of Florida.

The Florida royal palm is found in southern Florida.

The Brazilian rubber tree of the Amazon River basin is the chief natural source of pure rubber.

Horse Chestnut flowers

Quaking Aspen leaf

Lichen growing on a Pitch Pine branch

Staghorn Sumac leaflets

Balsam Fir with bright green spring growth

Apple blossoms in May

Smooth bark of Quaking Aspen trunks

Flowering Dogwood branch

Heart-shaped leaves of Linden (Basswood) in summer

Sugar Maple leaves in autumn

Flowering Dogwood (cultivated pink variety)

Red Maple samaras, or seeds

Ripe fruit on an Apple tree

American Elm leaves in autumn

Sharp needles of Blue Spruce

Staghorn Sumac leaves and berries

American Beech leaves in autumn

Cluster of male flowers on Eastern White Pine

Black Oak leaves

Witch Hazel flowers in November

Bear Oak leaves in spring

Evergreen leaves of American Arborvitae

Box Elder leaves and samaras

Bright fruit of European Mountain Ash

Bebb Willow catkins in spring

Ginkgo leaves

Gray Birch leaves in summer

Northern Red Oak leaf in fall

Red Maple leaves in autumn

New spring leaves on a Bear Oak

Trees of the American Desert

A **desert** environment is very dry. Very little rain falls, and the sun can be blazing hot during the day. At night, it can get quite cold. This is not a good environment for many kinds of plants. True desert areas are found in the American West and Southwest, such as the Sonoran Desert in Arizona and California, the Mohave Desert in California, and the Chihuahuan Desert of New Mexico and Texas. There are no lush forests of maples and oaks in these deserts and no shady stands of flowering dogwoods or magnolias.

A few species of desert plant do grow tall enough to reach tree height. The **Joshua tree**, a kind of **yucca** plant, grows in the Mohave Desert. It has pointed, sword-like leaves, and its trunk divides into branches. Joshua trees may reach a height of 35 feet (10.5 m).

The leaves of Joshua trees and other yuccas are thick, and they can store water better than the thin leaves of a forest tree (like a maple). Botanists call these thickened leaves **succulent leaves**. Succulent leaves are usually covered by a waxy coat, which helps keep the leaves from drying out.

Chocolate is made from the powdered seeds of the cacao tree, a native of Trinidad, Tobago, Mexico, and Central America.

Other desert trees include the **yellow paloverde** and **blue paloverde trees**. Both are small, shrubby trees with yellow flowers. Both species have tiny leaves that grow only when there is rainy weather. When the desert drought returns, the leaves fall off.

Banana trees look like palms, but they are not related to the Palm family. Many varieties are cultivated throughout the tropics and southern United States.

The Joshua tree is a member of the Lily family. It is well adapted to a desert environment.

Correction opposite: *New spring leaves on a White Oak*

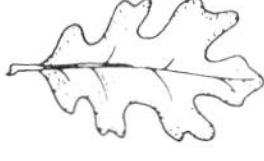

Giant Saguaros—Trees of the Desert?

Tall, bristly **saguaro cacti** grow in the Saguaro National Monument in the Sonoran Desert in Arizona. These impressive cactus plants can grow up to 50 feet (15 m) tall, with a main trunk or stem, and several "arms" branching upwards. Some are about 200 years old, and a big saguaro can weigh several tons. But are they really trees?

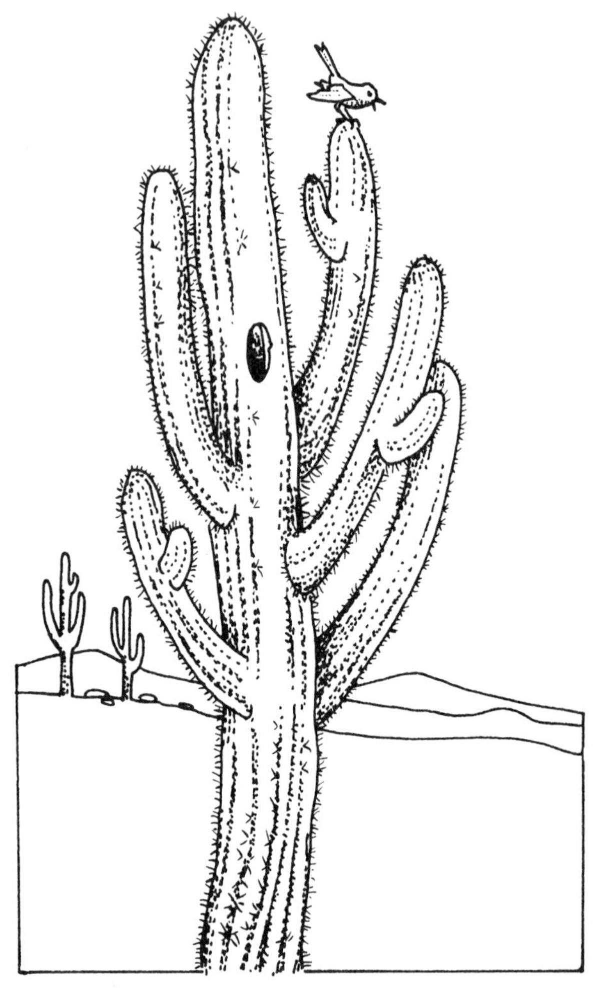

The giant saguaro cactus of the American deserts provides homes for birds just like forest trees do.

Most botanists don't classify the saguaro cactus as a tree, because it doesn't have flat, wide leaves like a forest tree. But botanists do know that the **sharp, woody spines** of a cactus are actually reduced, modified leaves. The spines don't look like leaves at all, but they do have an important purpose. They keep animals from trying to eat or chew the juicy, succulent stems of the saguaro!

These big cacti are the tallest plants in the Sonoran Desert, and their branching arms provide homes for desert birds, just as forest tree branches do. The saguaro has been called the king of cacti. Perhaps we could also nickname it the "tree of the desert."

The large white flowers of the saguaro cactus are the state flower of Arizona. These big beautiful blossoms are visited by many kinds of desert insects.

Trees provide all kinds of medicines, like salicylic acid (that's in aspirin) from willow bark, to dull a headache.

Unfortunately, the saguaro cactus may be one of the first plants to suffer from our thinning **ozone layer**. Botanists have found that some saguaros are losing their spines, and turning brown. And they think this may be due to increased **ultraviolet rays** from the sun.

Along the Meandering River

The banks along a river and the edges of a pond are often shaded by large, healthy trees. That's because there is plenty of water for the roots of the trees, even if there hasn't been much rain. Trees may grow quite abundantly next to large lakes, rivers, streams, and ponds. The zone of land along a river or lake where trees and other plants grow thickly is called a **riparian habitat**.

The lime tree of Great Britain and Europe is related to North American basswoods. It is not *a relative of the citrus trees grown in orchards that produce limes.*

This riparian land is the home of a variety of wildlife. Deer, foxes, songbirds, owls, and many other animals use riparian land for nesting sites or dens, and for feeding. The dense trees and plants give animals a protected travel-lane, or "corridor," where they can move without being easily seen. A riparian habitat should always be preserved, so that wildlife can feed, travel, and nest in safety.

More Rain in the Forecast

A **tropical rain forest** is a warm, wet world. Most rain forests are near the Equator, and they get plenty of rainfall each year. There are rain forests in Central and South America, Africa, Southeast Asia, many Pacific islands, and in northern Australia. But not all rain forests are hot.

The Olympic Peninsula in the state of Washington receives a lot of fog and rain, creating a **temperate rain forest** of huge hemlock and spruce trees along the Pacific coast. Some botanists think that this unique forest extends as far south as northern California and even as far north as southeastern Alaska.

A temperate rain forest does not contain as many species of tree as a tropical rain forest.

Cloud forests grow in the high mountains of the tropics. Here temperatures are cooler and mists cover the forest canopy. Strange plants, colorful birds, and beautiful butterflies inhabit these forests.

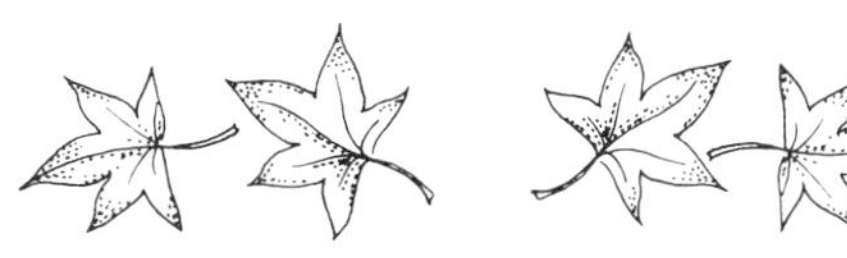

By early November, the branches of deciduous trees—like these oaks and maples—have lost their leaves.

— 4 —

Fall

Autumn brings chilly winds and sparkling frosts to many parts of the world. This is a time of changes—especially for trees and other plants. The leaves of many deciduous trees will turn brilliant red, orange, or yellow, and all the leaves will fall from the twigs.

As you look at the bare branches, you know it may be five months before you will see green leaf buds again. But fall is harvest time, too. It's a season of seeds and a time to hunt for nuts and berries.

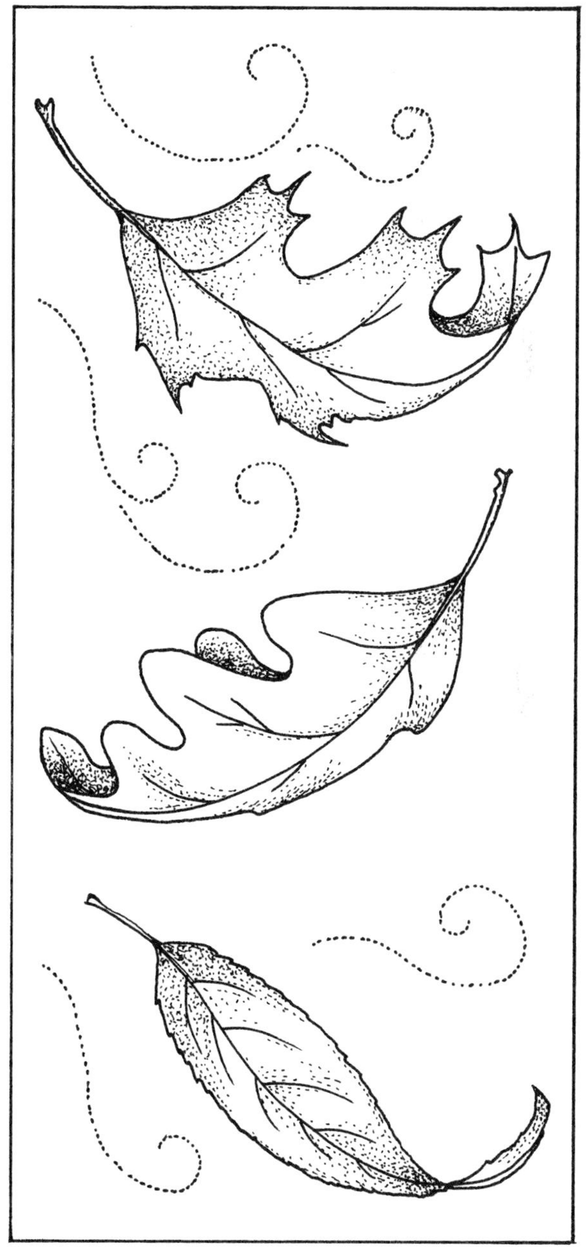

Once the leaves start to fall, branches will be bare in just two or three weeks.

Losers Win

Each autumn, throughout Canada, Europe, northern Asia, and much of the United States, many trees lose their leaves. Trees which shed their leaves each year are often called **broadleaf** trees or **hardwoods**. Botanists call them **deciduous trees**. Red maple, sugar maple, quaking aspen, weeping willow, and northern red oak are all examples of deciduous trees.

Before the leaves fall from most deciduous trees, they may turn beautiful colors—scarlet red, bright orange, and golden yellow. The colors of autumn leaves are so attractive that tour buses travel the mountains of New England each year, so that people can view the hillsides of brilliant orange and red.

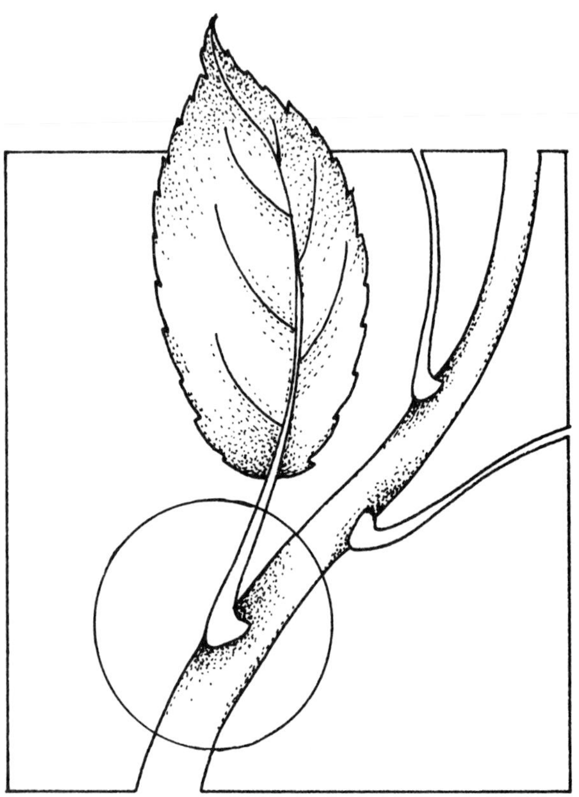

Leaves separate from the trees at the place where the base of the petiole meets the twig.

In North America, leaves turn their brightest colors in October. These colors only last for about two or three weeks. Red maples turn bright red or red orange. Sugar maples turn yellow or orange. The leaves of weeping willows and quaking aspens become yellow and yellow gold. In most of the eastern United States, the Pepperidge tree leaves turn dark red. This is the best time to take a hike in the woods or a stroll in your city park to see these bright fall leaves.

A Change in the Air

What makes leaves turn from green to bright red or yellow? Why do the leaves fall off?

It's because several things are happening at once.

Days become shorter as winter nears. That means there are fewer hours of sunlight for photosynthesis.

Cooler temperatures cause growth activity to slow down.

A new layer of cells grows to separate the leaf petiole from its twig, like a wall.

Water and sugar flowing out to the leaves slows down and then stops.

Cold temperatures occur only in the more northern States and Canada, so that's where the brightest colors are.

It's Photosynthesis Again!

As the days get shorter and colder, **photosynthesis** slows down and then stops. During photosynthesis, a green-colored substance called **chlorophyll** is created. Chlorophyll is the **pigment** (coloring) which makes plants look green. Less and less

The seeds (called samaras) of a sugar maple hang from the branches in clusters. Samaras from red maples are often red.

Magnificent Maples

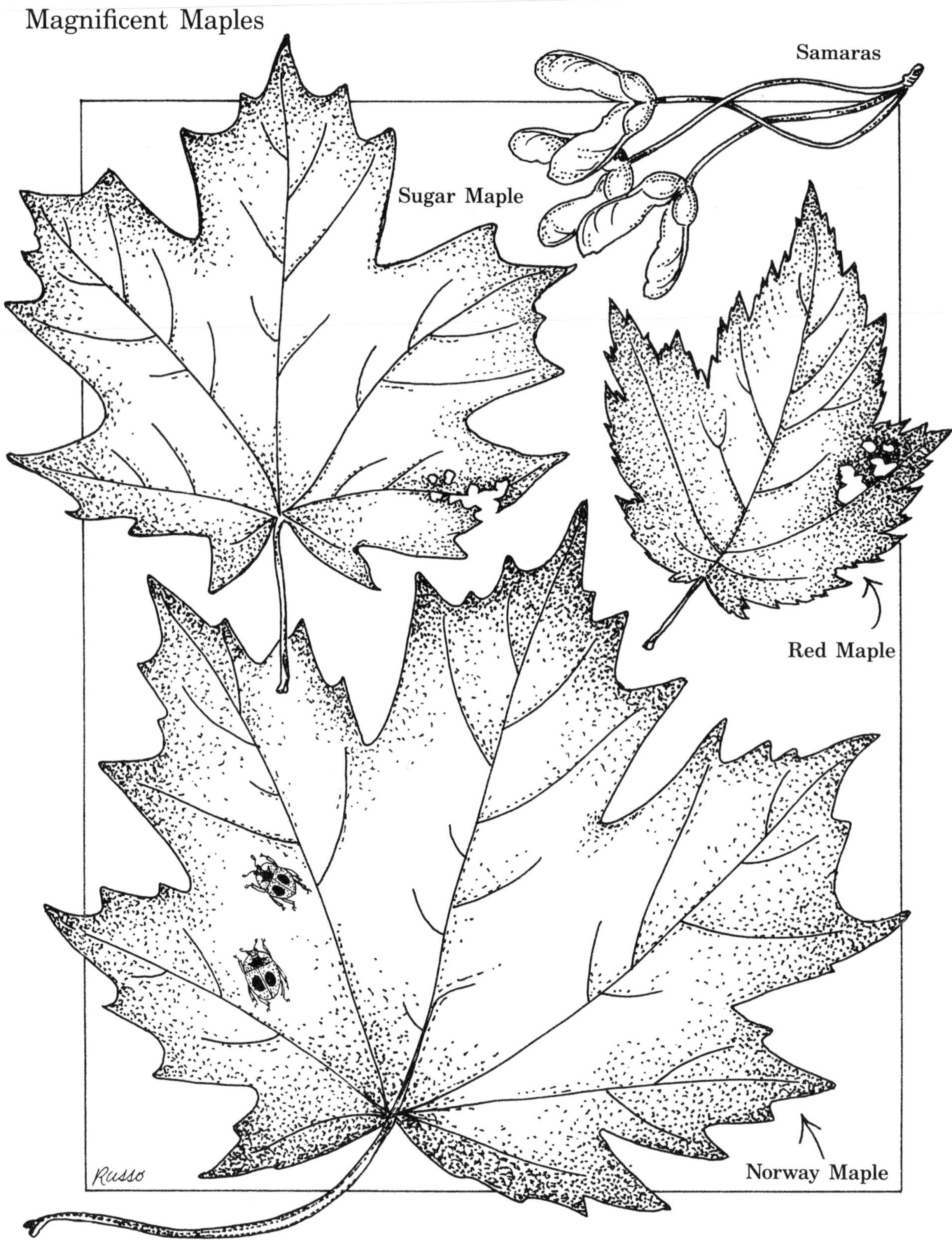

green chlorophyll is made—and what's left of it finally disappears.

When the green has gone, other pigments get a chance to "show their colors." The coloring pigments that make a leaf look red or orange are the same pigments which make a rose look red or a carrot, orange.

These other colors were there all along. Now that the chlorophyll is gone, you can see these other pigments.

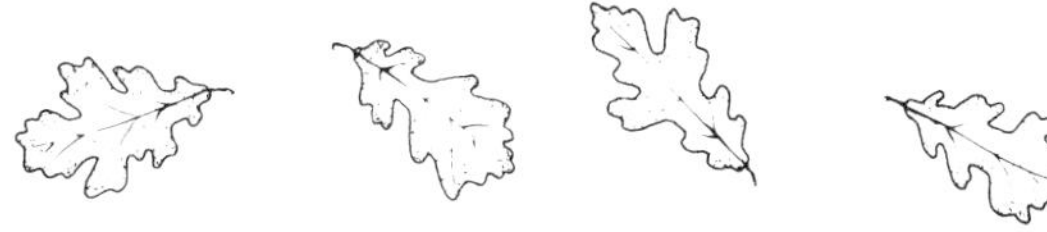

How Many Leaves Fall from One Tree?

Thousands. Anywhere from about 50,000 leaves fall from a small tree to more than 400,000 leaves from a big tree.

Star Attractions

Magnificent Maples

The leaves of the red maple turn brilliant red in the fall. The leaf petioles, and even the seeds (called **samaras**), are usually red, too. Red maples grow wild in the eastern U.S. and southeastern Canada, but nursery-grown red maples are planted along streets across North America. They're also used for **landscaping** around houses, schools, and office buildings.

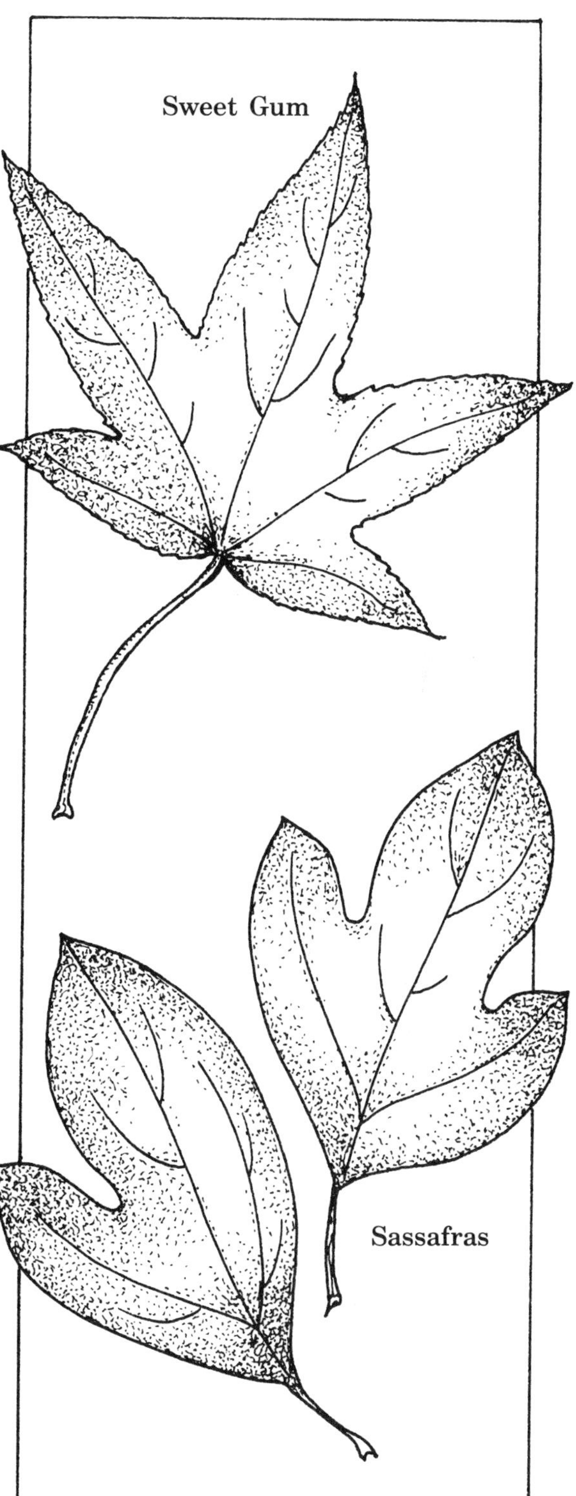

Sweet gum and sassafras leaves turn orange and red in the fall.

The leaves of the **sugar maple** turn bright yellow and yellow orange. This is the tree that maple syrup comes from. Sugar maples are sometimes planted as shade trees along streets. Their leaves are bigger than those of the red maple, and they don't have as many "teeth" along the edge. The sugar maple leaf even adorns the Canadian flag!

Norway maples turn bright yellow also. Their leaves are usually bigger and wider than those of the sugar maple. Norway maples don't grow wild in North America—they're a species native to Europe and Scandinavia. However, nurseries grow Norway maples and sell them for planting near buildings or along streets for shade.

Wonderful Willows

The leaves of **quaking aspen**, a member of the **Willow family**, turn yellow gold in the autumn. The leaf petioles are long and flat, so every time a breeze blows, each leaf flutters and quivers. That's why it's called the quaking aspen, or the trembling aspen. A whole hillside of bright yellow aspen leaves fluttering in the wind is a beautiful sight, and a favorite scene for outdoor photographers to shoot.

Eastern cottonwood and **bigtooth aspen**, also members of the Willow family, have **flat petioles** too. The leaves of both these trees quiver in the wind, and turn yellow or yellow gold in the fall.

Other members of this family include **black willow** in the eastern U.S., **Pacific willow** of the western U.S. and Canada, and **Bebb willow**, a small tree found across most of the northern states and much of Canada. These are native wild species of willows.

The **weeping willow**, with its graceful, drooping branches, is planted across much of North America, but it originally comes from China.

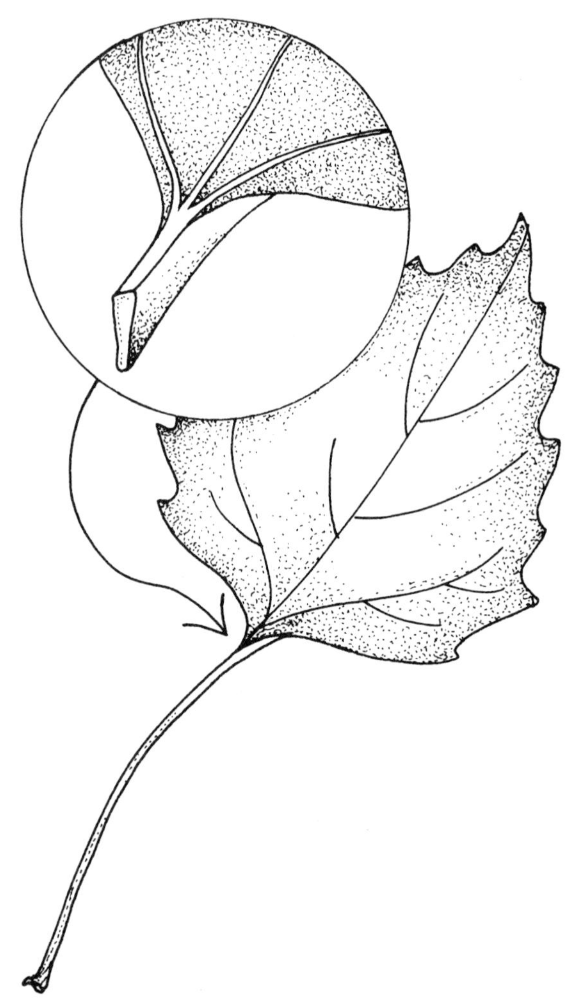

The petiole of an aspen leaf is flat. This causes the leaf to flutter and quiver in any breeze.

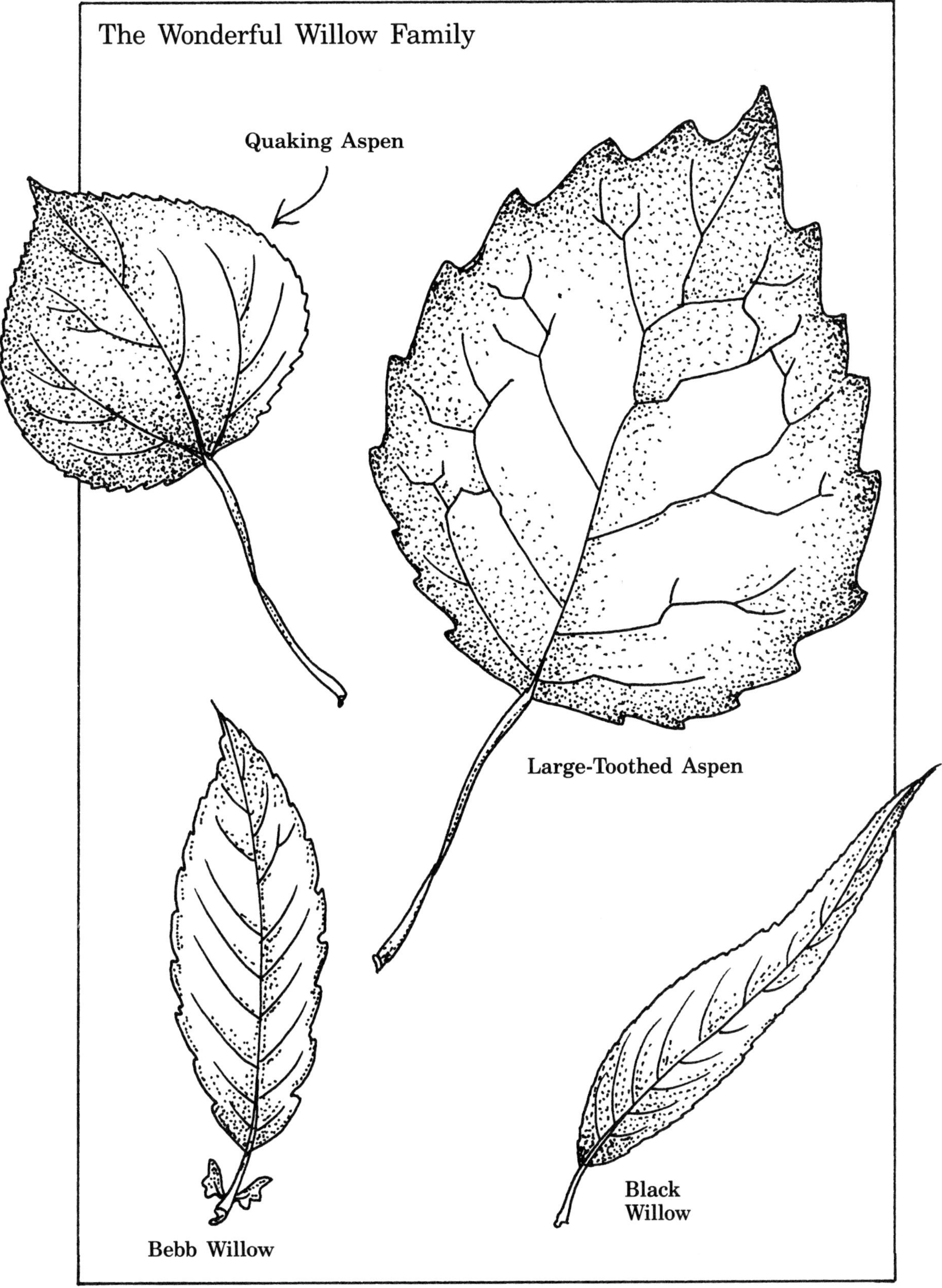
The Wonderful Willow Family
Quaking Aspen
Large-Toothed Aspen
Bebb Willow
Black Willow

In North America, the boiled twigs and bark of **willow trees** has been a **folk remedy** for headaches and arthritis. The willow actually contains a compound closely related to aspirin!

The leaves of all these trees turn yellow or yellow gold in the fall.

One of the first flags of the American colonies had a design with a pine tree in the center of the flag.

The Bright Stuff

Here are a few other species of deciduous tree which have bright leaves in the fall.

Species	Leaf Color	Range
Paper Birch	Yellow	Most of Canada and northern U.S.
Staghorn Sumac	Red	Quebec and Maine, south to Smoky Mountains, west to Great Lakes
Sassafras	Orange, red	Most of eastern half of U.S.
Tulip Tree	Yellow	Most of eastern half of U.S.
Sweet Gum	Orange, reddish purple	Southeastern U.S.
American Elm	Yellow	Eastern half of U.S.
Northern Red Oak	Dull red, orange	Most of eastern half of U.S. (southern red oak, a separate species, grows in southeastern U.S.)

Here and There

In North America, the bright colors of autumn can be seen across much of Canada and the United States. The leaves of the **Pepperidge tree** (also called **black tupelo**) turn deep, dark red—whether the tree is one that grows in Maine or in Tennessee. And flowering dogwood leaves become red purple, whether the dogwood grows in Connecticut or farther south in North Carolina. Quaking aspen leaves are yellow each fall throughout most of Canada, in the mountains of Utah, or "back East" in the hills of Vermont.

Falling Leaves

Hanging On

Some deciduous trees hang on to their leaves, even after they have turned color. **American beech** trees often retain some of their dried out, papery leaves all winter long. As every chilling wind drifts by, these dry leaves rustle and shudder in the cold air. Many **oaks**, especially younger ones, keep some dry brown leaves on their twigs throughout the winter months.

Leaf Litter

Each year, a new layer of dead leaves settles onto the forest floor. The older layers rot and decay, but the newly fallen leaves add to the crunchy brown blanket called **leaf litter**. Sometimes leaf litter is very thick or deep. This thick layer of dead leaves helps to protect roots from freezing temperatures. It also provides homes and feeding areas for many types of small animals.

Hordes of tiny insects live in the leaf litter, and mice and voles search in the leaves for seeds and sprouts. Salamanders and snakes hunt through the leaves for insects and earthworms. Birds such as ruffed grouse, woodcock, and ovenbirds nest on the ground, and need a good layer of leaves to hide their nests. The leaf litter rots as mold, fungus, and insects slowly eat it or destroy it.

The ovenbird builds its nest on the ground, where leaf litter can conceal the nest.

The dry, papery leaves of American beech often cling to the twigs all winter.

Autumn frost decorates the edges of fallen oak leaves. Layers of dead leaves several inches deep may blanket the forest floor.

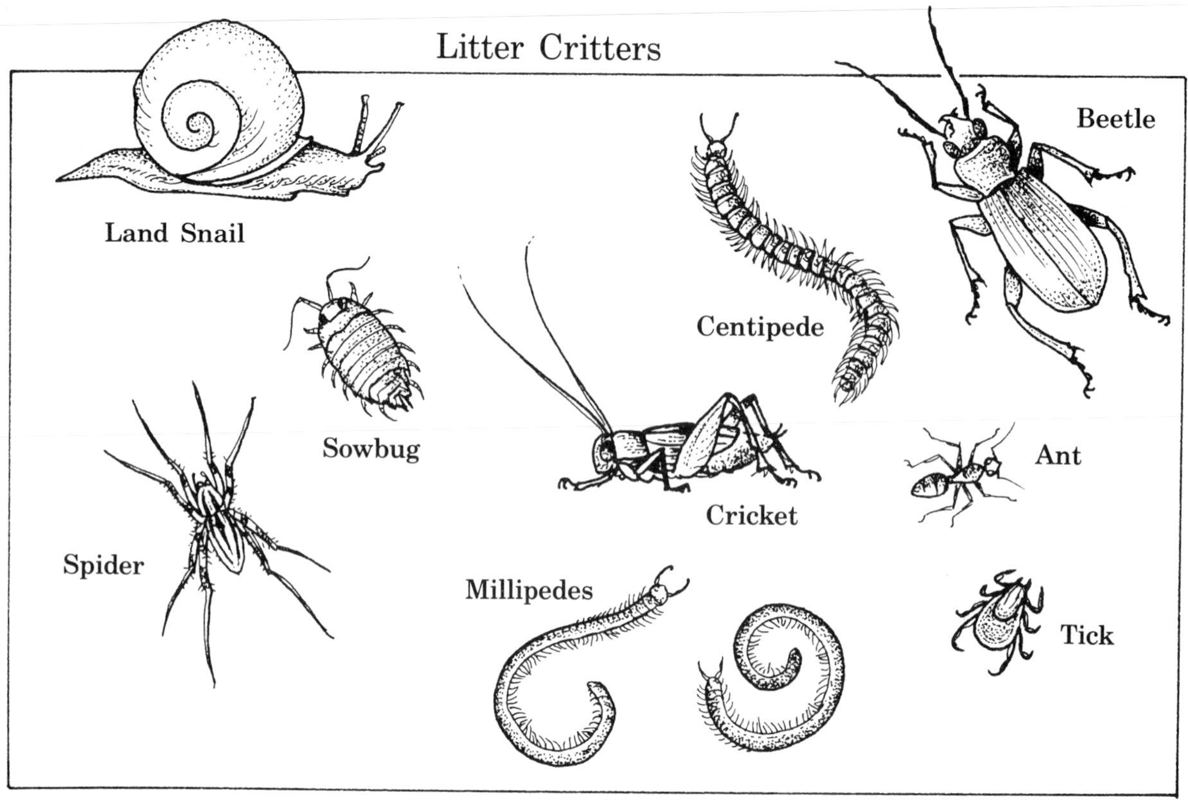

Litter Critters

You can easily find out what kind of tiny creatures are living in leaf litter. Put a big handful of old rotting leaves in a large, clear plastic container. Pretty soon you'll be able to see insects and other tiny animals crawling around in their new surroundings. You'll be able to look right in at these "litter critters" as they move about. You can also spread the leaves out on a large piece of white paper, so that the creatures are easy to see.

Here are some of the animals you might find in your pile of old leaves—ants, sowbugs, slugs, beetles, crickets, ticks, centipedes, salamanders, spiders, millipedes, snails, or mites.

Wear gloves when handling the leaf litter—there could be some prickly **nettles** or spiny **raspberry stems** mixed in, or even a **tick** or **mite** which may bite.

Time to Investigate

Cracks and Crevices

Now that the leaves have fallen, it's a good time to investigate the **bark** on **trunks** of trees. The outer bark of a tree is mostly made up of **dead**

cells. Sometimes this bark has an interesting surface texture. A few species of tree, like **American beech**, have smooth bark, but most trees have bark that is rough, flaky, or furrowed. These rough textures are great places for insects to hide.

By closely inspecting the trunk, you might find a specimen to add to your insect collection. **Moths, beetles**, and **ants** are frequently found crawling on or hiding in the cracks and crevices of bark. Even in the fall, many of these insects are still around.

Shagbark hickory, found in most of the eastern states, has very scaly, shaggy bark. Inspect the crevices of this bark and you're likely to discover some hiding insects or even a **cocoon** or **insect eggs**.

Looking for Lichens

On the trunks of many trees, you can find **moss** growing, and sometimes small plants called **lichens**. Moss and lichens don't hurt the tree at all, and they are fascinating to study. Botanists have found that some lichens are more abundant where there is the least amount of air pollution. Trees growing in the country have more lichens than trees in a large city with polluted air. Lichens can cover so much of a trunk, it's hard to see what the bark underneath actually looks like!

A magnifying glass helps to reveal the interesting shapes of mosses and lichens that grow on tree bark. Sometimes these plants look like miniature forests, forming tiny hills and valleys as they grow over the rough bark.

Autumn Harvest

Each fall, millions of **apples** are harvested across North America. We eat apple pie, apple strudel, apple sauce, and around Halloween we drink hot spiced cider. **Apple trees** are grown in orchards, backyards, and farm fields throughout the United States and Canada. There are many different varieties of apples—Red Delicious, Russets, McIntosh, Winesap, and Granny Smith, to name only a few. The most apples are grown in the former Soviet Union—almost twice the amount grown in the U.S. each year.

People everywhere are fond of apples. We use this familiar fruit as a symbol of health, goodness, and friendship. The apple even turns up in our everyday speech.

"There are no bad apples here."

"Now he's really upset the apple cart."

"That's as American as apple pie."

"They're as different as apples and oranges."

These lichens are growing right on the bark of a red maple tree. Lichens grow very slowly and these will not harm the tree at all.

Ready to be picked, these Golden Delicious apples are bound to be sweet and juicy.

Apple trees can grow as much as 30 feet (9 m) tall. But trees grown in orchards are much smaller—only 10 to 20 feet (6 m) tall. They are carefully trimmed and pruned so they don't grow very high. That's because it's much easier to pick apples from a small tree than a big one!

The Well-Travelled Apple

The first apple trees probably grew wild in Europe or Asia. Cultivation (the planting and care) of apple trees spread throughout Europe and England hundreds of years ago. North America did not have apple trees until about 300 years ago—when English settlers brought apples with them to the colonies. The first apple trees in America were probably planted in the Boston, Massachusetts, area.

Royal Gala apples, developed in New Zealand orchards, are now becoming a popular fruit in North America.

Johnny Appleseed (1774–1845)

John Chapman, a young man from Massachusetts, was single-handedly responsible for increasing the number of apple trees in colonial times. Known by the nickname **Johnny Appleseed**, he travelled across Pennsylvania, Ohio, Indiana, and Illinois, planting apple trees and collecting apple seeds.

John Chapman began this work when he was 18 years old, and he continued to plant and grow apple trees during his entire life. He loved flowers and animals and all natural things, so he planted not just apple trees, but herbs such as catnip and wintergreen, also. He taught many country people how to cultivate and care for plants.

Corks and cork boards are made from the waxy, spongy bark of the cork oak tree, a native of Europe.

Not Just Apples and Oranges

Across North America, trees provide delicious food. Aside from many varieties of apples, **orange** trees are also grown in the southern states and California. **Peach** trees, first grown in China over 4,000 years ago, are also cultivated here. Some other trees grown in North America give us these fruits:

Pears	Grapefruit	Apricots
Plums	Nectarines	Cherries

Fruit trees grown in orchards or groves are trimmed, so they are often less than 15 feet (4.5 m) tall. But they're still trees.

Nutcracker Sweet

Every autumn, stores and markets sell a variety of nuts, including pecans, walnuts, and almonds. All of these nuts are great to eat right from the shell, or baked in breads, cakes, muffins, and even candy.

The **pecan tree** is native to the southeastern U.S. One pecan tree can produce as much as 500 to 600 pounds (225 to 270 kg) of nuts in one year. Texas and Georgia together produce most of the pecan nuts sold in the United States. These nuts have thin shells, so they're easy to crack. And they're great when used to make pecan pie and holiday breads and cookies.

The **black walnut** is also a native wild tree, growing in many of the eastern states. It's often planted as an ornamental tree, and it can reach

Walnuts, pecans, and almonds are good examples of food crops grown on trees.

These oak acorns are eaten by many kinds of birds.

Shagbark hickory nuts are protected by a thick husk or hull. The nut inside the shell is a favorite food of small animals.

100 feet (30 m) in height. The nuts of black walnut are so good that they were eaten raw and roasted by the American Indians and planted at George Washington's home estate. Some of the walnuts sold in stores are **English walnuts**, a different species from our native black walnut tree, but cultivated in California.

American Beech Seeds and Hulls

Butternut trees, also called **white walnuts**, grow northward into New England and southern Quebec. A native forest tree growing about 50 feet (15 m) tall, it has nuts which are usually as good as those of black walnuts. Butternut shells are oval, like pecans, and the green husks are sticky.

Almonds are related to peach trees, and they are originally from Asia and the Mideast. Almond trees bloom very early in the spring, so they need a mild climate. California probably cultivates more almond trees than any other state.

Food for All

Trees provide plenty of fruit and nuts for people, but forest trees also produce an abundant supply of food for wildlife.

Acorns from **oak trees** are eaten by quail, grouse, wild turkey, wood ducks, blue jays, and nuthatches. In California and the Southwest, the acorn woodpecker collects and even stores acorns for future use. Throughout much of the U.S. and southern Canada, there are many different species of oaks which provide food for wildlife.

The seeds of **American beech** are called **mast**, or **beechnuts**. This tree is found in most of the eastern states and southeastern Canada. The three-sided beechnuts are eaten by wood ducks, grouse, chipmunks, black bears, porcupines, and squirrels.

Shagbark hickory, paper birch, tulip tree, and all the maples also bear nuts or seeds which birds and other animals feed on.

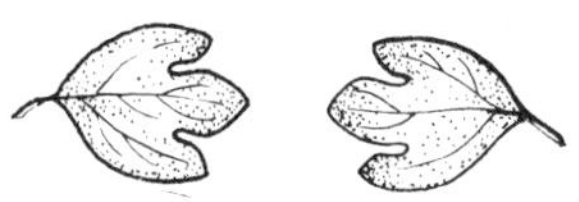

The legendary Robin Hood was supposed to have used a bow made from the common yew of Great Britain.

Robins, cardinals, and other birds like to eat the dark red berries that grow in clusters on staghorn sumac.

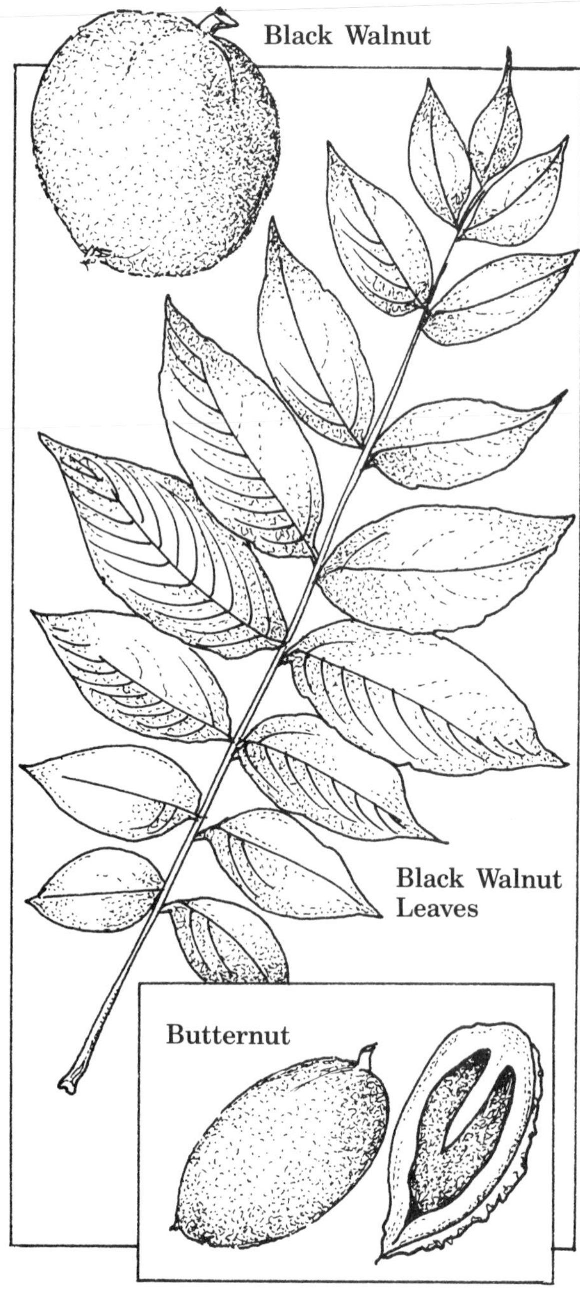

Fruit Is Fine

The fruits of the **wild black cherry**, and those of the **pin cherry** and **choke cherry**, are eaten by robins, catbirds, evening grosbeaks, and cedar waxwings. Deer, skunks, and raccoons feed on the fruits of the **common persimmon**, which grows in the Southeast. **Sumac berries** are another fruit favored by many species of birds. **Staghorn sumac** berries often grow in colonies or clumps, and they attracts bluebirds, cardinals, and mockingbirds.

Use your nose to identify a tree. The freshly cut twigs of black cherry have an unpleasant, bitter smell you won't like!

Sassafras roots were sent to England by the first American colonists more than 200 years ago. The roots were thought to be a useful medicine for many illnesses.

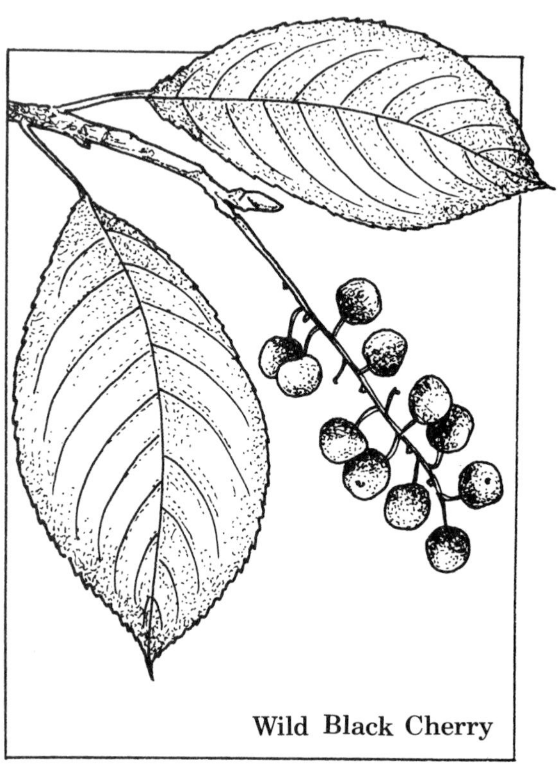

The main food of the koala bears of Australia is the leaves of eucalyptus trees.

Hawthorn berries are also a favorite food of wildlife. There are at least 100 different species of hawthorns in North America. Almost all are small trees, and many are planted near homes and office buildings for their beautiful flowers.

Fruit and nut trees produce food for wildlife from the end of summer through fall and winter. A great variety of songbirds, game birds, and small mammals depend on this natural food supply to get them through a cold winter.

Two Evergreens of the South

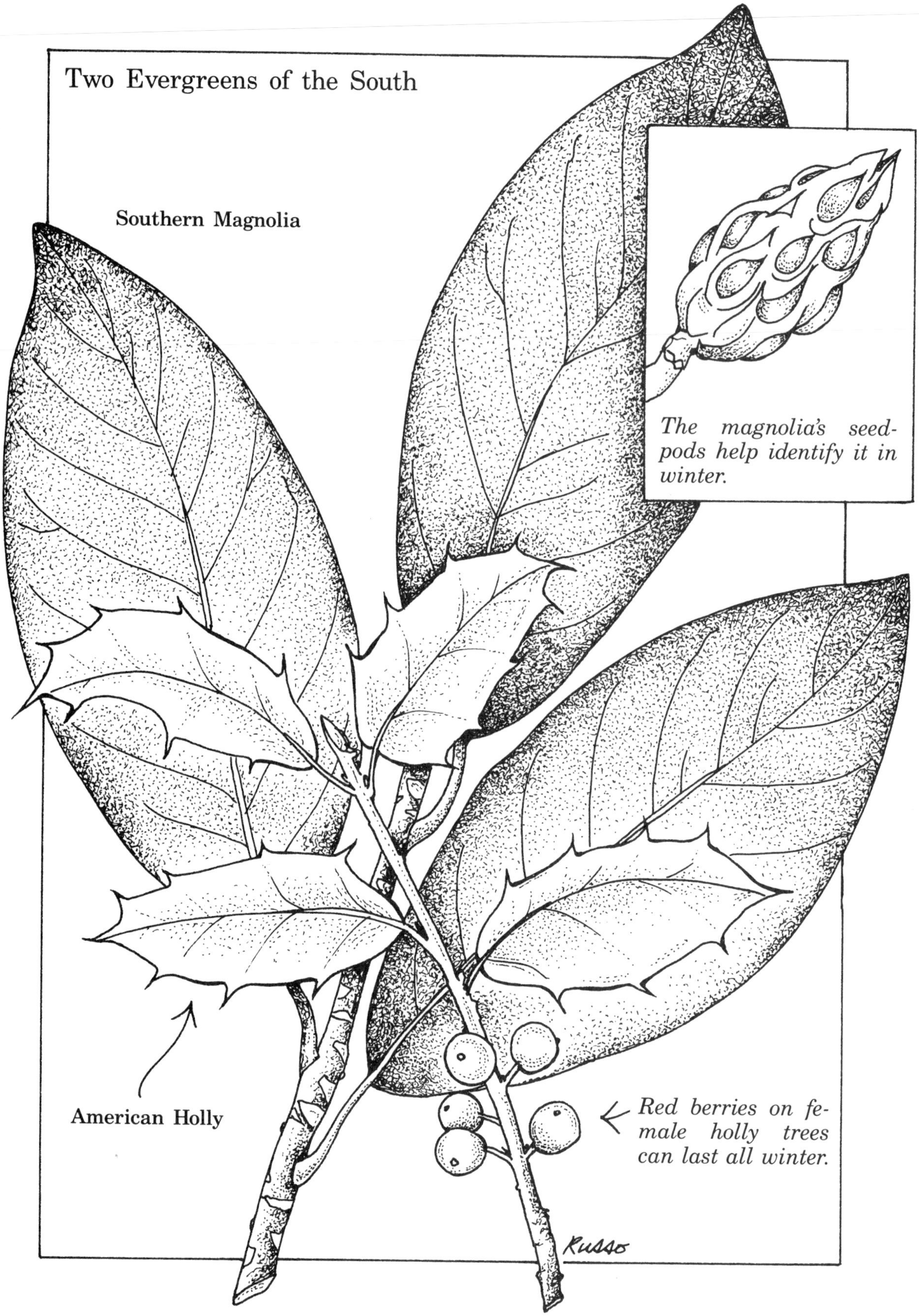

Southern Magnolia

The magnolia's seedpods help identify it in winter.

American Holly

Red berries on female holly trees can last all winter.

Russo

— 5 —

Winter

Frost, snow, and ice are familiar to many people around the world, during the winter months. Even if you live in a warm climate, like southern Florida, it's cooler now than it is during the summer. There are also fewer hours of sunlight each day.

Colder temperatures and a shorter day both affect the life of a tree. **Deciduous trees** have already lost their leaves and they survive through the winter in a **dormant** condition. During dormancy, **photosynthesis** slows down or nearly stops.

Even the evergreen trees, such as pine and spruce, become dormant in very cold climates. Some of these trees may still absorb rain or moisture, but growing activity slows down or stops.

The Norfolk Island pine is often grown as a small potted houseplant. But in its native island habitat near New Zealand, it may grow 70 feet (21 m) tall!

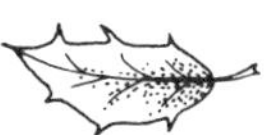

Evergreens

Trees which have green leaves throughout the year are called **evergreens**. Many different species of evergreen tree are found across North America.

Most northern evergreens include species of **pine, spruce, fir**, and **hemlock**. In the southern states, plenty of pines grow, but there are also **evergreen oak trees**.

Here are some evergreen trees (besides pines) that grow where winters are mild.

Live Oak—Southwest and Texas

Canyon Live Oak—California

Southern Magnolia—Southeast

American Holly—Southeast up to southern New England

Orange Tree—planted in groves, mostly in Florida and California

---

Worldwide, there are over 400 species of tree in the Holly family, but not all of them have evergreen leaves.

The leaves of trees in the Pine family are often thin and pointed, like the sharp "needles" of this blue spruce.

All evergreens have green leaves on them throughout the year, but they don't keep the same set of leaves. Older leaves fall off each year, but they are replaced by new ones. The leaves never fall off all at once, like the leaves of a deciduous tree. There are always green leaves on an evergreen tree, but during the winter months there may be fewer leaves altogether.

The Pine Family

Members of the **Pine family** have thin or flat leaves that are often called **needles**. The leaves are long, thin, and needle-like on some species, but short and sharply pointed on others.

Here are some evergreen members of the Pine family found in North America.

Eastern White Pine (Northeast)

Loblolly Pine (Southeast)

Pinyon Pine (Southwest)

Sugar Pine (California)

Black Spruce (Northeast and Canada)

Eastern Hemlock (Northeast)

Balsam Fir (Northeast and Canada)

Douglas Fir (western U.S. and Canada)

White Spruce (Canada and northern U.S.)

Most members of the Pine family are evergreen. Some exceptions are **tamarack** and **larch** trees, common in the North and in Canada. The needles of these trees turn yellow in the fall, and all the needles fall off.

Some members of the Pine family are native to other countries, but are grown here in nurseries and planted across North America.

Norway Spruce—from Europe

Mugho Pine—from the mountains of Europe

Scotch Pine—from Scotland and northern Europe to Siberia

The **blue spruce** grows wild in the Rocky Mountains, but it's also grown in nurseries and planted in the eastern states, well away from its native habitat.

Many different species of pine, spruce, and fir are often called **"Christmas trees."** But that's *not* a scientific name! It doesn't refer to any particular species of tree.

The sap from Brazilian rubber trees has been used to make rubber for a long time. Over 100 years ago, scientists found that the sap—called latex—could be heated, and treated with sulphur, to make it harder and tougher.

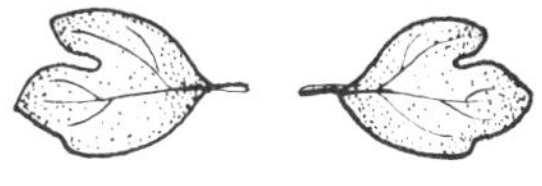

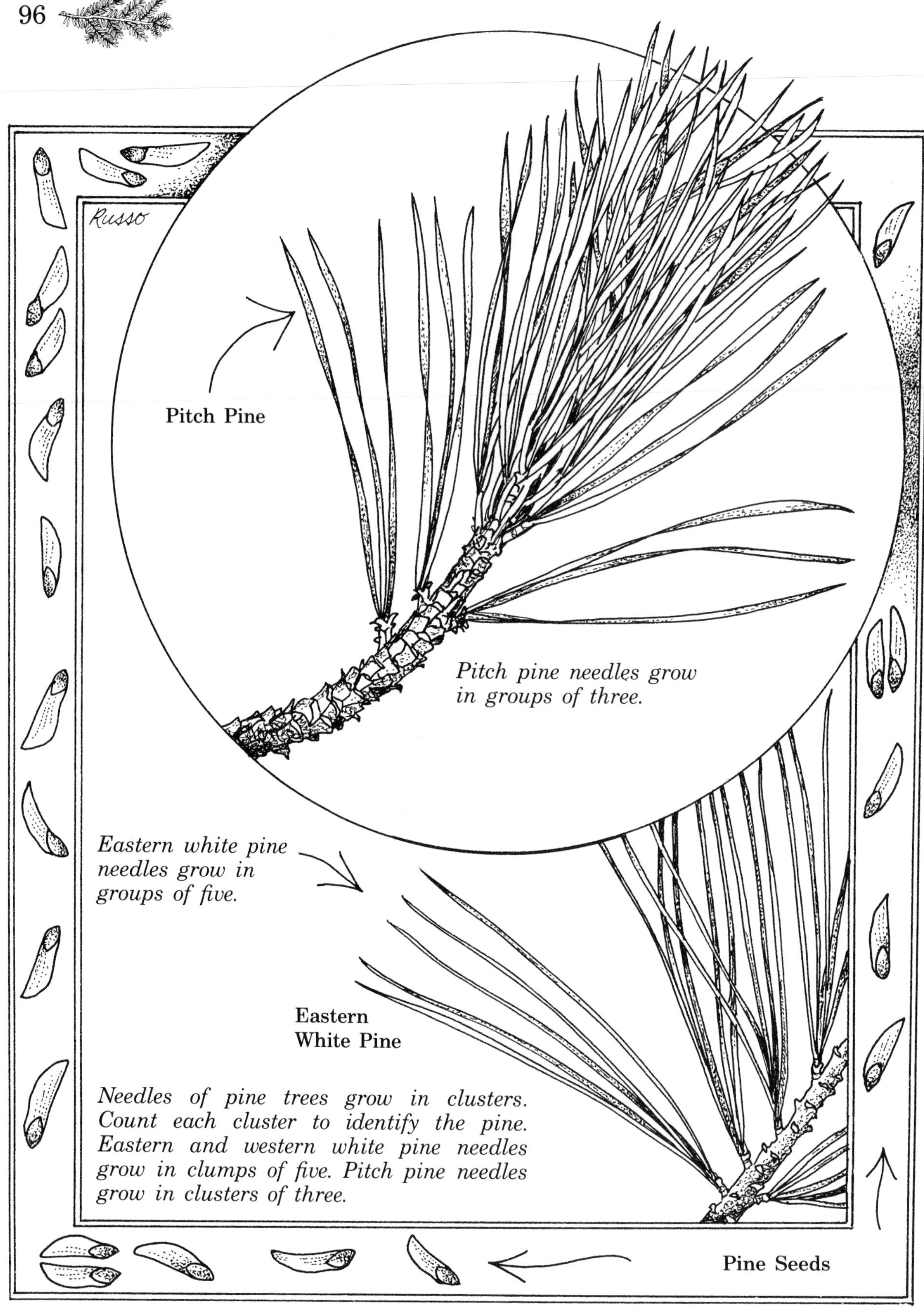
Russo
Pitch Pine
Pitch pine needles grow in groups of three.
Eastern white pine needles grow in groups of five.
Eastern White Pine
Needles of pine trees grow in clusters. Count each cluster to identify the pine. Eastern and western white pine needles grow in clumps of five. Pitch pine needles grow in clusters of three.
Pine Seeds

Count Your Pine Needles

The thin, needle-like leaves of pine trees grow in **clusters** on the twigs. You can identify many species of pines by counting the number of needles in each cluster.

Eastern white pine (Northeast) has five needles to a group.

Red pine (Northeast) has two needles to a cluster.

Longleaf pine (Southeast) has two *very* long (over a foot) needles to a cluster.

Lodgepole pine (West and western Canada) has two short needles in a group.

Pitch pine (Northeast south to the Great Smoky Mountains) has three short, stiff, slightly twisted needles to a group.

Cones in All Sizes

All members of the Pine family bear **cones** on their branches. Some cones fall to the ground in about a year, but others remain on the tree much longer. **Pitch pine** and **jack pine** retain their cones for over 10 years! Members of the **Pine family** are often called **conifers** because they bear cones.

Some cones are small—those of **eastern hemlock** are barely an inch long. But the cones on **sugar pine** are over a foot in length. **Fir tree cones** stand upright on their branches. Most **pines** and **spruces**, however, have cones that hang downward from the branch.

Young, new cones are greenish, and tightly closed up. Older cones become dry, turn brown, and open up to expose the seeds inside. When these ripe cones open, the seeds within fall out or are blown out by the wind. The seeds of most conifers have thin, papery wings to help them drift and travel in the wind. Each cone has plenty of seeds inside.

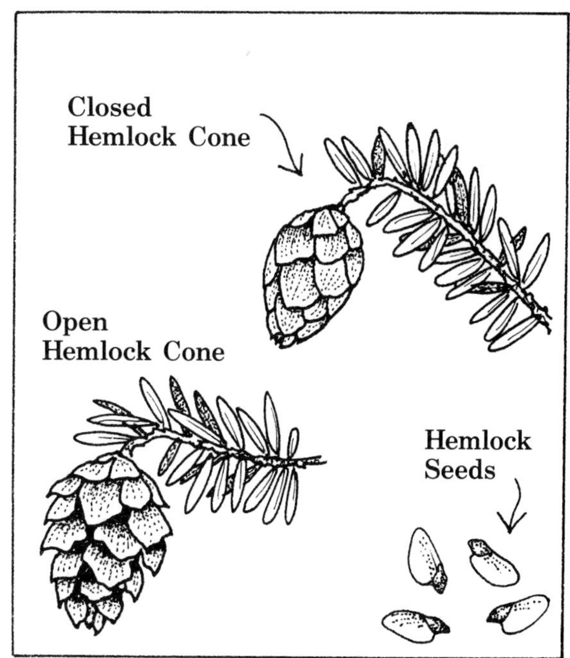

A young hemlock cone is closed up. But an older cone opens up to let its seeds fall out. Cones also close up when the weather is very damp.

In the American West and Southwest, **pine seeds** have been gathered and eaten by Native Americans for generations. The seeds from the **pinyon pine** are a favorite food, and are used today in cooking and baking.

The cones of eastern hemlock are small—about an inch long. Western hemlock looks very much like its eastern relative.

This great horned owl is one of many kinds of birds that like to nest or roost in tall evergreens.

Food for Wildlife

During wintertime in the Northeast, the seeds of **eastern white pine** and **pitch pine** are eaten by chickadees, crossbills, and nuthatches. The seeds of many other pines are eaten by doves, grouse, quail, pine grosbeaks, siskins, and pine warblers. Some of these birds can pry the seeds from the cones, using their beaks. Others eat seeds that have fallen to the ground.

Squirrels sometimes climb to the tops of pine trees, chew the cones from their branches, and let the cones fall to the ground. Then the squirrels can sit on the ground, taking apart each cone to get at the seeds. Porcupines, chipmunks, mice, ground squirrels, and even deer eat pine seeds.

Millions of eastern hemlock trees were once cut down for their bark, which provided an ingredient necessary for tanning shoe leather.

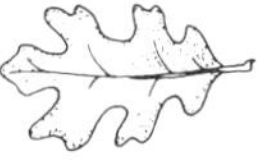

Evergreen Shelter

Trees in the Pine family provide plenty of food for wildlife. And they offer shelter, too. A **grove**, or **"stand,"** of pine, spruce, or fir trees makes a good place for wild birds to roost during winter storms. The dense growth of branches and leaves shelters the birds from wind and snow. Large birds, such as crows, hawks, and owls, perch high in the branches of tall conifers. The dark shadows close to the trunk help to hide these big birds.

Amber is the fossilized sap from prehistoric evergreen trees. Amber from Lebanon has been found to be about 100 million years old!

More Kinds of Evergreens

In the West, **redwoods, giant sequoias, Pacific yews**, and **western red cedar** are evergreen trees. **Cypress trees**, found in the West, and **junipers**, found across North America, are evergreens also. The blue berries of junipers and **eastern red cedar** (also a type of juniper) are a favorite food of bluebirds and cedar waxwings.

None of these trees belongs to the Pine family, but some, like redwood and cypress, have woody cones.

Around the House

Many kinds of evergreens are used for landscaping around our homes, schools, or parks. **American arborvitae, Scotch pine**, and **English yew** are grown in nurseries across North America for homeowners and landscapers to plant.

Common Landscaping Evergreens

These evergreens are used for landscaping around schools, houses, and parks.

Eastern Red Cedar

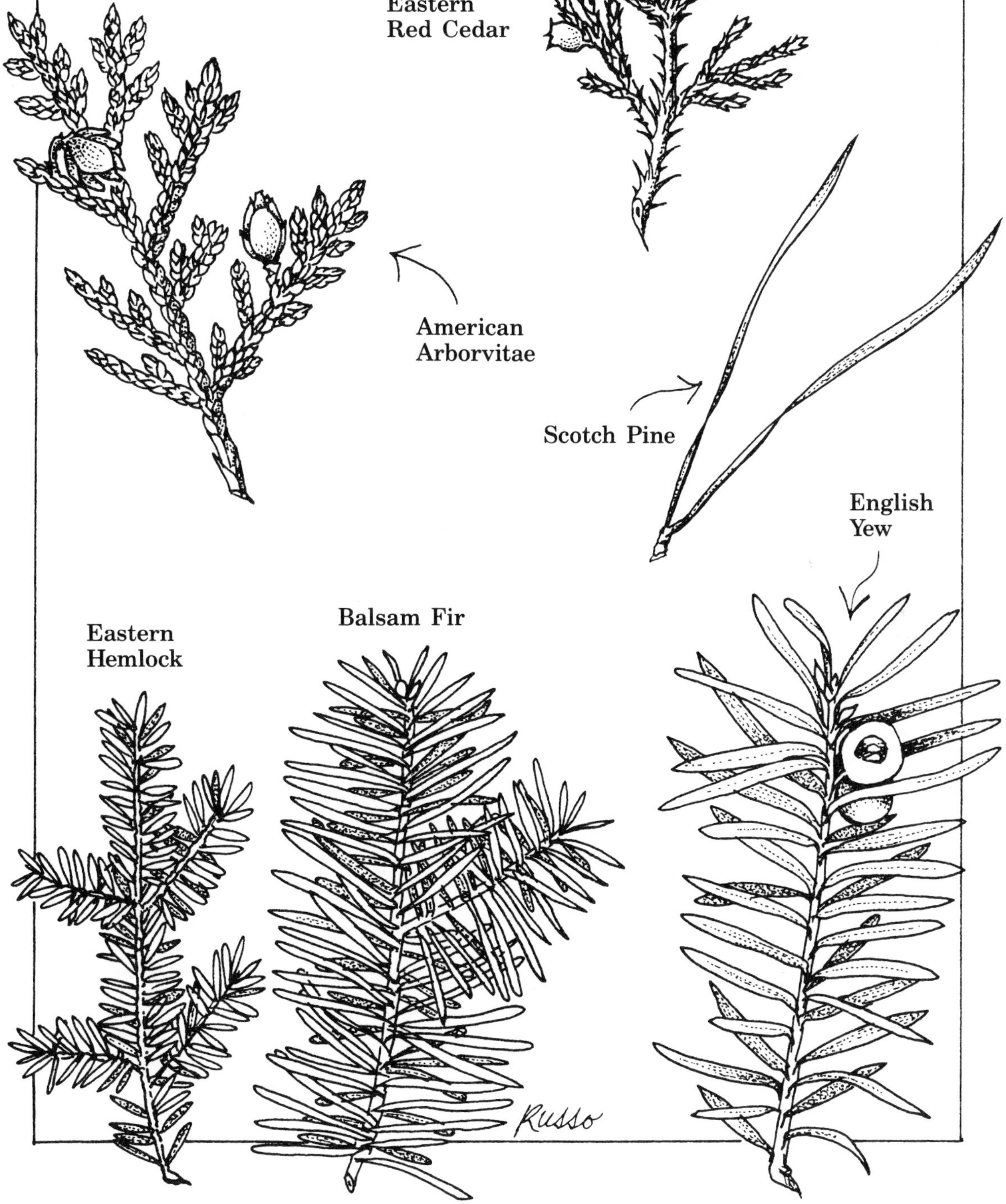

American Arborvitae

Scotch Pine

English Yew

Eastern Hemlock

Balsam Fir

Russo

Severe winter temperatures and the heavy weight of snow can crack and break some tree branches.

The Survivors

Trees growing in Canada, Alaska, the northern states, Scandinavia, and northern Russia have to survive very cold temperatures and difficult winter conditions. Both deciduous and evergreen trees are exposed to winter hardships.

The weight of snow can break off branches. Ice and severe cold can cause a trunk to split or crack. High winds can blow trees over or snap off large branches. Blowing ice particles can grind away at the bark, wearing away a tree's protective layer.

Constant winter wind can be harmful because it dries out the leaves by evaporating moisture. Trees in the Pine family have thin or narrow leaves. These shapes help keep them from drying out, because only a small area is exposed to the wind. The leaves of pines and other evergreens often have a waxy coating, which also helps to prevent loss of moisture to winds.

Colder and Colder

Below-freezing temperatures can damage a tree or even kill it. Different species of trees survive different amounts of freezing. A prolonged temperature of 15 degrees might kill a **live oak tree** living in the South.

But **eastern white pines** growing in northern Maine survive winter after winter of temperatures below zero! **White spruce, black spruce, quaking aspen**, and **paper birch** all withstand temperatures of 30 or 40 below zero, or even colder.

No Trees At All

No trees grow at the **North Pole** or the **South Pole**. The severe cold and constant drying winds make those places uninhabitable for any kind of

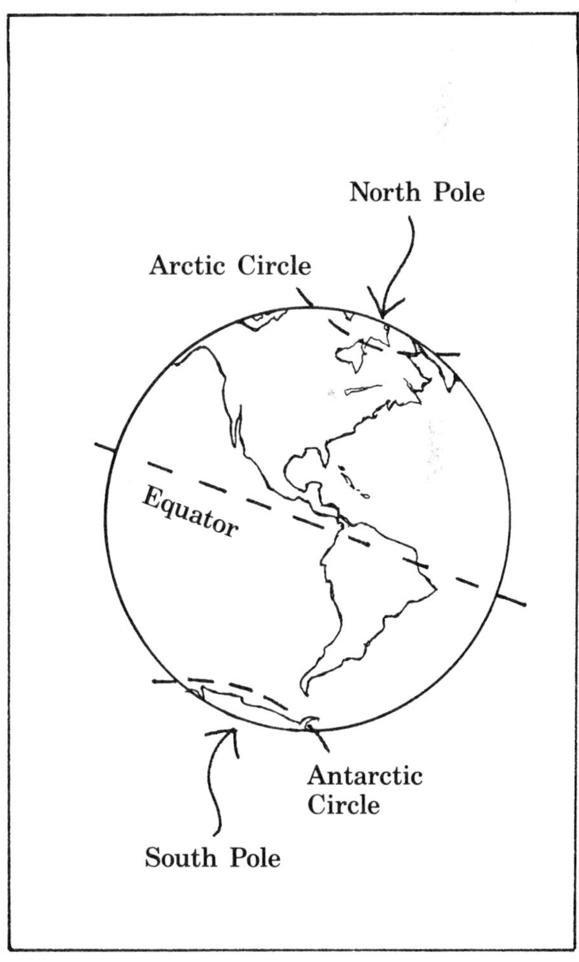

No trees grow at the North Pole or South Pole, and few trees grow much beyond the Arctic Circle.

tree. The soil above the **Arctic Circle** is frozen hard most of the year. Many kinds of small plants do grow in the Arctic, such as mosses, lichens, and even flowering plants, but trees do not grow much beyond the Arctic Circle. Some species that do survive in Arctic regions around the world are **larch, birch**, and **aspen**.

Beyond the **Antarctic Circle**, there's mostly just ice. Some lichens, fungi, and mosses grow in part of Antarctica, but there are *no* trees!

A pine growing near the timberline in the mountains may be stunted and misshapen.

The Timberline

No trees live at the tops of high mountains. The barren place at the top of any mountain (or north in the Arctic) where trees have stopped growing is called the **timberline**, or **tree line**. Trees that grow near or at the timber line in the mountains are often stunted, twisted, and misshapen. Their bark is sometimes worn away by strong winds, which force particles of sand or ice against the trunk. It's not a good climate for trees at all.

Winter Activities

Waxed-Paper Leaves

Did you end up with a lot of extra pressed leaves that you collected in the summer or fall? Do you have leaves that you can't identify, but think they're too interesting to throw away? You can make some great winter window decorations, using your extra leaves. All you need is some waxed paper and the use of an iron.

Here's what to do.

- Lay a thin cotton cloth, rag, brown paper, or newspaper on the ironing board.
- Place a sheet of waxed paper on the cloth, and arrange your pressed leaves on it.
- Put a second sheet of waxed paper on top, so that you have a "leaf sandwich."
- Cover the waxed paper with another thin cloth or brown paper. And use a *warm* (not hot!) iron to seal the waxed sheets together with the leaves inside. Move the iron around, pressing down evenly.

Always ask your mom or dad to help you heat up the iron. Remember to unplug the iron as soon as you're done!

When you finish ironing the waxed paper, you can tape your leaf decoration to the window. Or you could cut the paper into shapes, hang them *near* a window, or even hang them from your Christmas tree!

This is also a good way to preserve the bright yellows and reds of fall leaves a little longer.

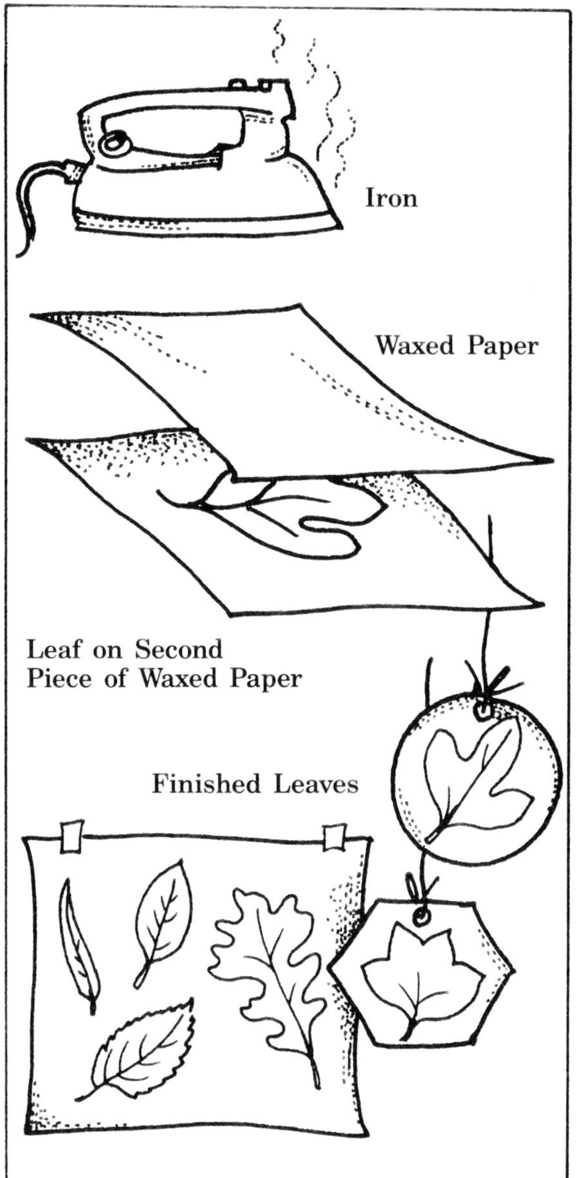

Waxed-Paper Leaf Decorations

Stringybark, red gum, silver dollar gum, ironbark, and ghost gum are only a few of the strange names given to Australia's eucalyptus trees.

Finding the Indoor Forest

You don't have to go outdoors to look for trees! Trees are beautiful, and people like to grow trees indoors in pots, where they can be seen all the time.

How many indoor trees can you find? Here are some places to look: a large shopping mall, the building where your mom or dad works, your dentist's office, the public library, and your school's main office.

Even if you watch television news, you might see a potted tree in the background of the news room!

Here are a few trees commonly grown in pots.

Norfolk Pine—an evergreen

Indian Rubber Tree—big, shiny, rounded leaves

Benjamin Fig (*Benjamin ficus*)—dark green, shiny leaves

Bonsai Trees—dwarf, tabletop-size trees

None of these trees ever grow large, because they are kept in pots and are pruned or trimmed. **Bonsai** trees are very small, because their branches and roots have been carefully pruned for many years. *Bonsai* is a Japanese word for trees that have been kept small this way. Evergreens, like pines and junipers, are often grown as bonsai trees.

How many indoor trees can you find in your neighborhood?

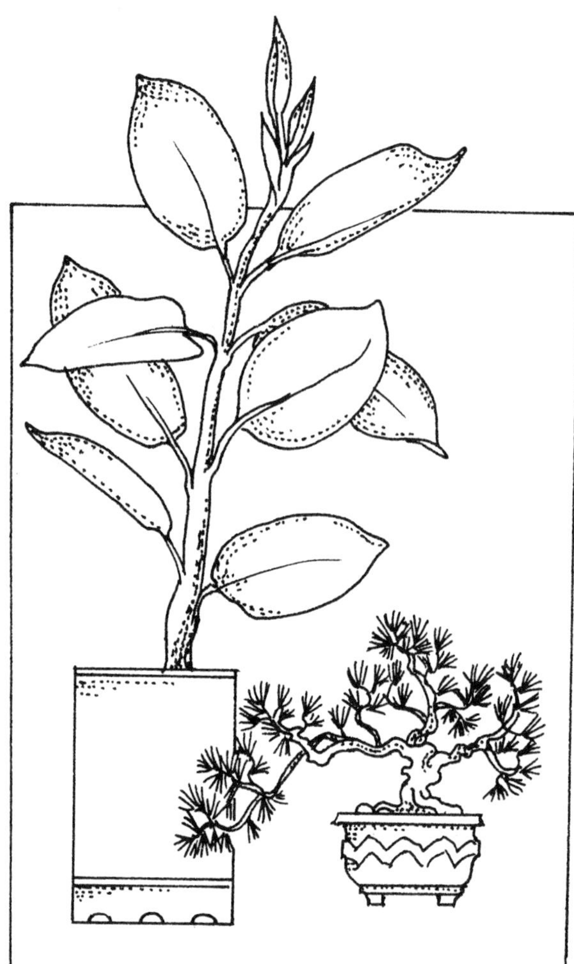

Tree grown in indoor pots, like the rubber tree plant and the bonsai pine, never reach full size.

The Corner of Elm and Maple

Here's a detective game you can play when you're traveling with your mom or dad, riding the school bus, or looking at a town map.

How many streets can you find that are named after trees? Here are a few street names from towns near the author—Elm Street, Maple Avenue, Birch Court, Chestnut Street, Juniper Knoll, Oak Ridge, and Sumac Lane!

The aspen of Great Britain, Europe, and Scandinavia have beautiful yellow gold leaves in the fall, just like the quaking aspen of North America.

How many streets in your town are named after trees? Why do you think they have these names? Finding the answers could be part of a class project!

The wood of the English oak was used in the construction of the Mayflower, *the ship that brought early colonists to America.*

Be a Budding Botanist

Since you *don't* live above the timberline yourself, you've probably got plenty of trees to look at during the winter. But how can you identify deciduous trees without their leaves? Just look for the **buds!**

Buds are an excellent clue when trying to identify trees in winter. These buds were formed at the end of the **growing season**—they're waiting for spring, when they'll open up into leaves or flowers. The shape and size of the buds will help you decide what tree it is. Each bud is protected by an outer coat of scales. Some buds are covered by several scales, but some have just one scale.

Here are some buds to look for this winter.

The buds of **American beech** are honey gold and *very* pointy.

Flowering dogwood buds face upward, with a point at the top—like an onion!

Willow trees have buds that hug the twig closely, and are covered by a single scale.

Hawthorn buds are nearly globular (completely round).

You can also identify a leafless tree by its bark, thorns, or remaining fruit or seed pods. Here are some clues to look for.

Peeling, chalky white bark identifies a **paper birch**.

Sycamore bark has large, smooth, peeling flakes in shades of green, brown, and grey.

Long, sharp thorns on a small shrubby tree tell you it's a **hawthorn**.

The buds of American beech are very pointed.

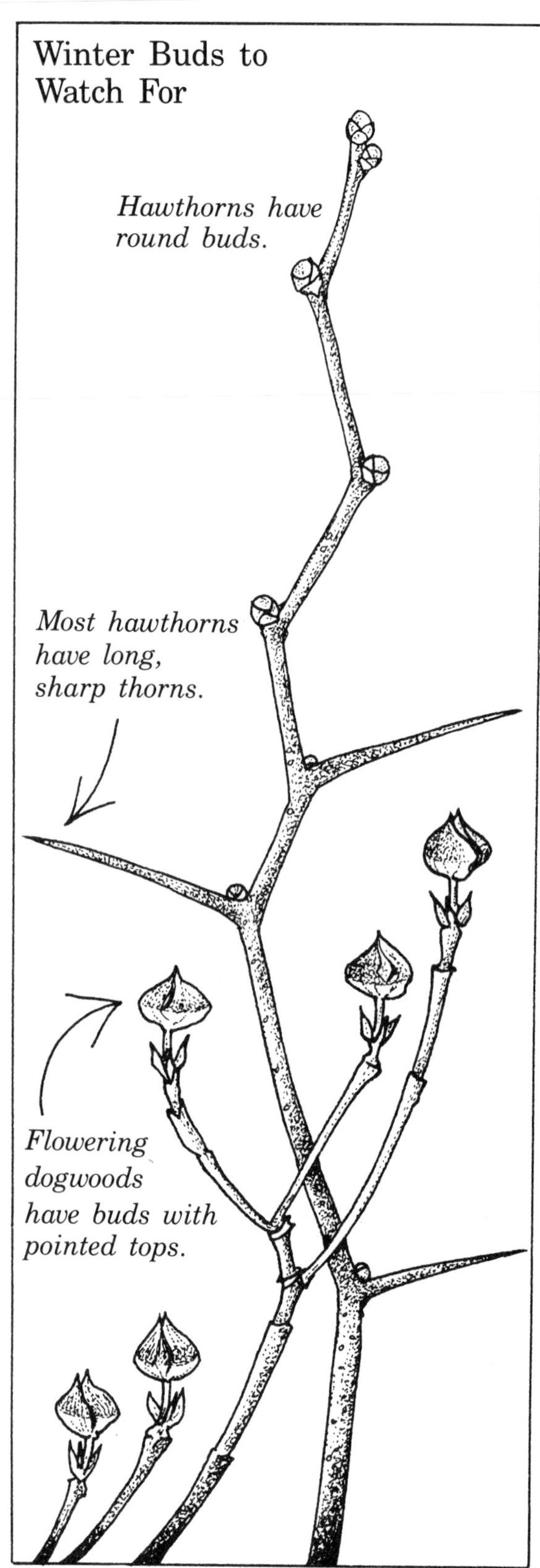

Staghorn sumac has fuzzy twigs and clusters of fuzzy dark red berries.

Time for Tag

Once you think you've identified a tree by its bark, thorns, or buds, tie a tag on it! It's easy to cut an **identification tag** from plastic or waxed milk cartons. Write the date and the name of the tree on your tag, using a marker that won't wash off during the winter. Tie the tag to a low branch, or around the trunk, with string. When the leaves come out in the spring, you'll be able to see if your guess was right.

You'll probably be able to identify several leafless trees around your school or home. It's a guessing game that makes waiting for spring easier, and it sharpens your observation skills. Tagging is a great outdoor project for a group of your friends or a school science club.

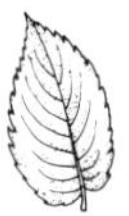  

The huge karri tree, a type of eucalyptus from southwestern Australia, rivals the American redwood in size.

Paper birch, also called canoe birch, has white, chalky bark.

You can count several holes in the old red maple snag to the right. Woodpeckers and chickadees use hollow trees like this for nests.

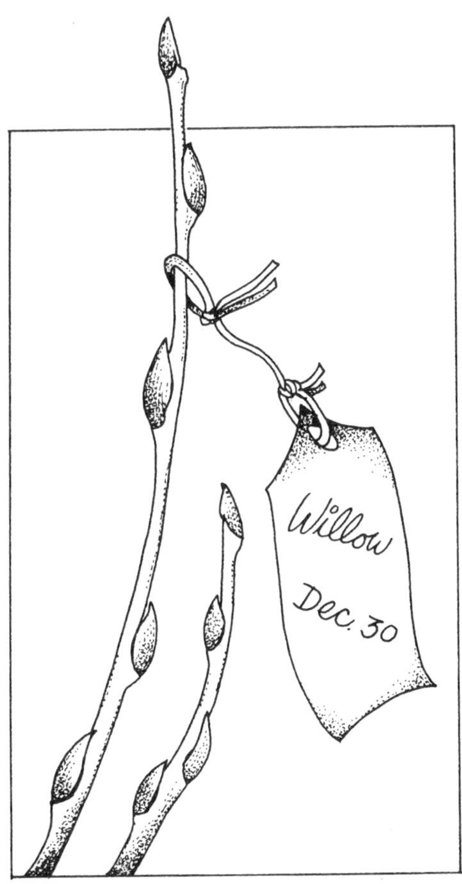

Tag a tree in winter with your guess about its identification. Watch for its leaves in spring to see if your guess was correct.

A Hole in One

As spring approaches, dead, decaying trees are just as interesting to observe as living trees. That's because many species of bird use hollow, rotting trees for nesting sites. These decaying trunks are called **snags**.

Rotting snags will attract woodpeckers, nuthatches, titmice, chickadees, and tree swallows. They all nest in hollow snags. Even larger birds, such as wood ducks, screech owls, and kestrels look for snags to nest in.

Warm, spring weather is soon to come, and a rotting old tree trunk may become the site of new life. That's why it's important to leave some decaying tree trunks standing, instead of cutting them down.

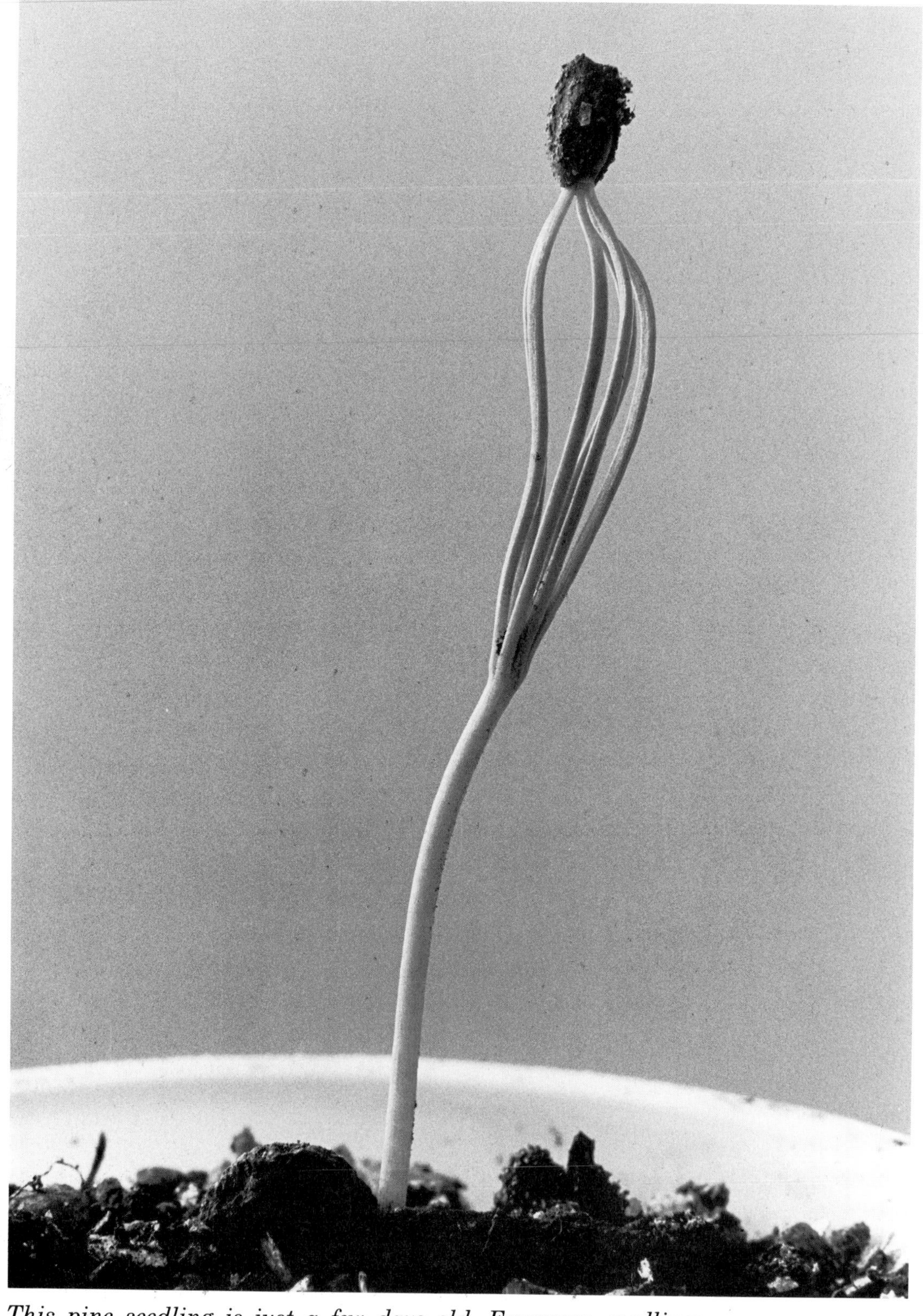

This pine seedling is just a few days old. Evergreen seedlings are grown on tree farms, at nurseries, and in forestry plantations.

6

Trees for People and People for Trees

Paper, Poles, and Pulp

Trees have always been a vital, valuable resource to people. For many hundreds—even thousands—of years, Native Americans used trees to make canoes, construct birch-bark boxes, weave baskets from strips of hickory and ash wood, and build covered lodges.

But when Colonial settlers arrived in North America, they cut down vast forests to supply England with poles for ships' masts and for other building lumber. They also cut down trees to create open farm land and to build towns. Most of those huge forests of enormous trees, known as **virgin timber lands**, are gone forever.

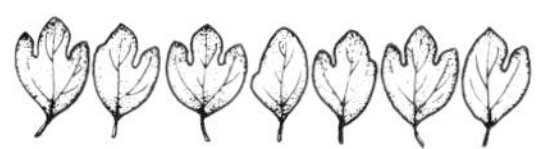

Australia has well over 500 species of eucalyptus trees, and many, such as the blue gum and ironbark, are grown in California.

Larch, or tamarack, trees are grown on tree farms. They have thin needles like pines, but the needles are short, and they are not evergreen.

Today, we cultivate groves of trees for **food**—apples, pears, cherries, walnuts, and oranges, for example. We search for trees that might provide **medicine**, such as the Pacific yew. We grow plantations of pines to cut for **lumber** to build houses, and we grow fields of larch to use for **poles** or **pulp**.

Also, most of our homes are made of wood and so is much of our furniture. Wood is used to build boats and to make the handles of axes and shovels.

Making Paper

Paper is made from the crushed pulp of trees, and from recycled paper products.

Paper also has been made from many different kinds of plants, not just trees. About 4,000 years ago, Egyptians used the fibers from tall slender reeds growing by rivers to make paper. That paper is called **papyrus**.

The first people to make paper from trees may have been the Chinese, about 1,800 years ago. They used the shredded bark of mulberry trees. In Central America, the Mayan Indians pounded and flattened the bark of fig trees to make paper, over 1,500 years ago.

From the 1300s to the mid-1800s in Europe, and later in the New World, most paper was made from rags and cloth. Today, high quality paper is still made from cotton and linen cloth.

Look for Paper and Wood

You could make a long list of everyday items made from trees—newspapers, comic books, schoolbooks, paper towels, envelopes, cereal boxes, maps, computer paper, and wrapping paper, for instance.

Look for other uses of trees or wood products when you go to school or when you play with friends. There are all kinds of things—telephone poles, pencils, hockey sticks, railroad ties, Popsicle sticks, and baseball bats.

In some parts of the Amazon forests, over 280 different species of tree can be found growing in just a few acres.

The United States produces—and uses—more paper goods than any other country in the world. As the population of people grows, so does the demand for these paper and wood items. That's why we need to use recycled products whenever we can.

The Caribbean National Forest of Puerto Rico protects over 12,000 acres of tropical rain forest.

Recycle whatever paper products you can, and use recycled products.

Working for the Forest

Huge, beautiful forest trees are cut down every day because we need more house-building lumber, more wooden products, and more paper goods.

But even as you read this page, people across North America are studying and growing forest trees in order to preserve our natural woodlands.

Botanists examine the health and growth of trees, while entomologists collect and study insects that may damage leaves and bark. Workers at tree farms try different methods to grow better seedlings. A lot of people—from forest firefighters to park rangers—are involved in the effort to preserve the forests we now have.

They all know that we need to ensure the health of our older forests, and that we need to plant vast acres of tiny seedlings to start new forests. In the State of Maine alone, millions of tree seedlings have been planted by paper company workers.

Some forestry work requires a technical and scientific education, while other jobs require only some special hands-on training.

Also, meteorologists, teachers, tree-farm workers, botanical artists, entomologists, soil scientists, fire-tower wardens, chemists, conservationists, and environmental students all can play a vital role in protecting our forests and woodlands.

Over 60 million years ago, there were about 40 species of tree in the Redwood family. But today, there are only two in North America—the giant sequoia and the redwood.

Into the Future

Tall forest trees are like time machines. Their past may include surviving droughts and storms, and their lives may have spanned hundreds of years of human history. These trees may continue to grow into a future of yet unknown human discoveries—a future of tremendous forests that you and your friends will want to enjoy!

Tree Families

Here is a list of trees mentioned in this book. They are all listed according to their **family** classification. The **scientific (botanical) name** is given also. By looking at the botanical names, you can see how closely some trees listed here are related. The botanical names come from Latin and Greek words that usually help describe the plant. For example, the pinyon pine is *Pinus edulis*. The word *edulis* refers to the edible seeds of this pine.

Some trees are identified in parentheses as aliens. These are trees that grow naturally wild in other countries but are cultivated here in North America.

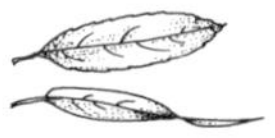

One **species** of tree may have many different common names. These additional names are given in parentheses.

Family	Common Name	Botanical Name
Yew	Pacific Yew (Western Yew)	*Taxus brevifolia*
	English Yew	*Taxus baccata* (alien)
Pine	Eastern White Pine	*Pinus strobus*
	Western White Pine (Mountain White Pine)	*Pinus monticola*
	Bristlecone Pine	*Pinus aristata*
	Sugar Pine	*Pinus lambertiana*
	Pinyon Pine	*Pinus edulis*
	Mugo Pine	*Pinus mugo* (alien)
	Red Pine	*Pinus resinosa*
	Lodgepole Pine	*Pinus contorta*
	Virginia Pine (Scrub Pine, Jersey Pine)	*Pinus virginiana*
	Ponderosa Pine	*Pinus ponderosa*

Family	Common Name	Botanical Name
Pine (continued)	Pitch Pine	*Pinus rigida*
	Loblolly Pine	*Pinus taeda*
	Longleaf Pine	*Pinus palustris*
	Scotch Pine	*Pinus sylvestris* (alien)
	Tamarack (Hackmatack, Eastern Larch)	*Larix laricina*
	Black Spruce	*Picea mariana*
	White Spruce (Skunk Spruce)	*Picea glauca*
	Red Spruce	*Picea rubens*
	Blue Spruce	*Picea pungens*
	Sitka Spruce	*Picea sitchensis*
	Norway Spruce	*Picea abies* (alien)
	Eastern Hemlock	*Tsuga canadensis*
	Western Hemlock	*Tsuga heterophylla*
	Douglas Fir	*Pseudotsuga menziesii*
	Balsam Fir	*Abies balsamea*
	Noble Fir	*Abies procera*
Redwood	Giant Sequoia	*Sequoia gigantea*
	Redwood	*Sequoia sempervirens*
Cedar or Cypress	Northern White Cedar (American Arborvitae)	*Thuja occidentalis*
	Western Red Cedar	*Thuja plicata*
	Arizona Cypress	*Cupressus arizonica*
	Incense Cedar	*Libocedrus decurrens*
	Western Juniper	*Juniperus monosperma*
	Eastern Red Cedar	*Juniperus virginiana*
Ginkgo	Ginkgo (Maidenhair Tree)	*Ginkgo biloba* (alien)
Palm	Florida Royal Palm	*Roystonea elata*
	Coconut Palm	*Cocos nucifera* (alien)
	Sabal Palm (Cabbage Palm)	*Sabal palmetto*

 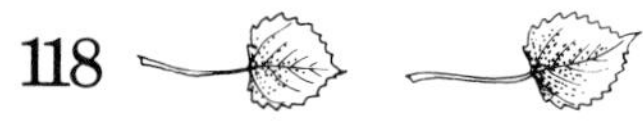

Family	Common Name	Botanical Name
Palm (continued)	California Fan Palm	*Washingtonia filifera*
Lily	Joshua Tree	*Yucca brevifolia*
Willow	Black Willow	*Salix nigra*
	Pacific Willow	*Salix lasiandra*
	Pussy Willow	*Salix discolor*
	Bebb Willow	*Salix bebbiana*
	Weeping Willow	*Salix babylonica* (alien)
	Eastern Cottonwood	*Populus deltoides*
	Quaking Aspen (Trembling Aspen)	*Populus tremuloides*
	Large-Toothed Aspen (White Poplar)	*Populus grandidentata*
Walnut	Black Walnut	*Juglans nigra*
	Butternut (White Walnut)	*Juglans cinerea*
	English Walnut	*Juglans regia* (England or Northern European)
	Shagbark Hickory	*Carya ovata*
	Pignut Hickory	*Carya glabra*
	Pecan	*Carya illinoensis*
Birch	Paper Birch (Canoe Birch, White Birch)	*Betula papyrifera*
	Yellow Birch	*Betula lutea*
	Black Birch (Sweet Birch, Cherry Birch)	*Betula lenta*
	Gray Birch	*Betula populifolia*
Beech	American Beech	*Fagus grandifolia*
	White Oak (Stave Oak)	*Quercus alba*
	Black Oak	*Quercus velutina*
	Northern Red Oak	*Quercus rubra*
	Bur Oak	*Quercus macrocarpa*
	Swamp White Oak	*Quercus bicolor*

Family	Common Name	Botanical Name
Beech (continued)	Post Oak	*Quercus stellata*
	Pin Oak	*Quercus palustris*
	Southern Red Oak	*Quercus falcata*
	Blackjack Oak	*Quercus marilandica*
	Myrtle Oak	*Quercus myrtifolia*
	Live Oak	*Quercus virginiana*
	Canyon Live Oak	*Quercus chrysolepsis*
Elm	American Elm (White Elm)	*Ulmus americana*
	Slippery Elm	*Ulmus rubra*
	Hackberry	*Celtis occidentalis*
Mulberry	Red Mulberry	*Morus rubra*
	White Mulberry	*Morus alba* (alien)
	Osage Orange	*Maclura pomifera*
	India Rubber Plant	*Ficus elastica*
Magnolia	Southern Magnolia	*Magnolia grandiflora*
	Bigleaf Magnolia	*Magnolia macrophylla*
	Saucer Magnolia	*Magnolia soulangeana* (alien)
	Sweet Bay	*Magnolia virginiana*
	Umbrella Magnolia	*Magnolia tripetala*
	Tulip Tree (Yellow Poplar)	*Liriodendron tulipifera*
Laurel	Sassafras	*Sassafras albidum*
Witch Hazel	Sweet Gum	*Liquidambar styraciflua*
	Witch Hazel	*Hamamelis virginiana*
Sycamore	American Sycamore (Planetree, Buttonwood)	*Plantanus occidentalis*
Rose	Common Apple	*Malus pumila* (alien)
	Southern Crab Apple	*Malus angustifolia* (alien)
	American Mountain Ash	*Sorbus americana*
	European Mountain Ash	*Sorbus aucuparia*
	Black Cherry	*Prunus serotina*

 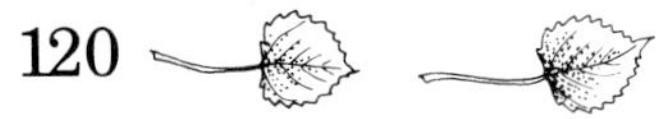

Family	Common Name	Botanical Name
Rose (continued)	Pin Cherry	*Prunus pensylvanica*
	Common Choke Cherry	*Prunus virginiana*
	Canada Plum	*Prunus nigra*
	American Plum	*Prunus americanus*
	Pear	*Prunus communis* (alien)
	Sweet Cherry	*Prunus avium* (alien)
	Almond	*Prunus amygdalus* (alien)
	Peach	*Prunus persica* (alien)
	Shadbush (Serviceberry, Juneberry)	*Amelanchier laevis*
	Scarlet Hawthorn	*Crataegus pedicellata*
Legume	Eastern Redbud	*Cercis canadensis*
	Honey Locust	*Gleditsia triacanthos*
	Black Locust	*Robinia pseudoacacia*
	Yellow Paloverde	*Cercidium microphyllum*
	Blue Paloverde	*Cercidium floridum*
Rue	Orange	*Citrus sinensis* (alien)
	Lemon	*Citrus limon*
	Grapefruit	*Citrus paradisi* (alien)
	Lime	*Citrus aurantifolia*
Ailanthus	Ailanthus (Tree of Heaven)	*Ailanthus altissima* (Asian)
Spurge	Brazilian Rubber	*Hevea brasiliensis*
Sumac	Cashew	*Anacardium occidentale* (alien)
	Pistachio	*Pistachia vera* (alien)
	Staghorn Sumac	*Rhus typhina*
	Poison Sumac	*Toxicodendron vernix*
Holly	American Holly	*Ilex opaca*
Maple	Sugar Maple (Rock Maple, Hard Maple)	*Acer saccharum*
	Red Maple (Swamp Maple)	*Acer rubrum*

Family	Common Name	Botanical Name
Maple (continued)	Silver Maple	*Acer saccharinum*
	Striped Maple (Moosewood)	*Acer pensylvanicum*
	Large-Toothed Maple	*Acer grandidentata*
	Box Elder (North American Maple)	*Acer negundo*
	Norway Maple	*Acer platanoides* (alien)
Horse Chestnut	Ohio Buckeye	*Aesculus glabra*
	Horse Chestnut	*Aesculus hippocastanum* (alien)
Linden	Basswood (American Linden, "Bee Tree")	*Tilia americana*
Cactus	Giant Saguaro	*Cereus giganteus (Carnegia gigantea)*
Dogwood	Flowering Dogwood	*Cornus florida*
	Pacific Dogwood	*Cornus nuttallii*
	Kousa Dogwood (Japanese Dogwood)	*Cornus kousa* (alien)
Tupelo	Pepperidge (Upland Tupelo, Black Gum, Sour Gum)	*Nyssa sylvatica*
Ebony	Common Persimmon	*Diospyros virginiana*
Ash	White Ash	*Fraxinus americana*
	Green Ash	*Fraxinus pennsylvanica*
Bignonia	Northern Catalpa	*Catalpa speciosa*

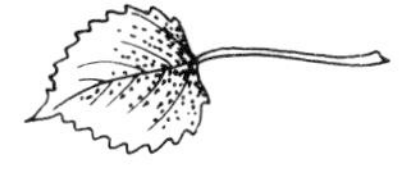  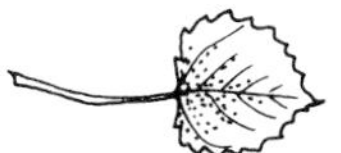 

Tree Terms

Term	How to Say It	What It Means
Arboretum	ar bor EE tum	A park, sanctuary, or protected property where trees are grown for study.
Bark	bark	The woody, outer covering of a tree trunk. It may be smooth or textured.
Blade	blade	The flat, wide part of a leaf.
Botanist	BOT ann ist	A scientist who studies plants.
Bract	brakt	Modified leaf that may look like a petal. The big, white "petals" of a flowering dogwood are really bracts.
Broadleaf	brawd leaf	A nonscientific name for most trees that lose their leaves each autumn. Deciduous tree.
Canopy	CAN o pee	The uppermost spreading, branchy layer of a forest.
Carbon Dioxide	CAR bon di OX ide	The gas that animals exhale. Plants need carbon dioxide to live.
Catkins	CAT kins	Long, dangling flowers found on birch and other trees. The flowers of willows. The fuzzy unopened buds of pussy willow.
Chlorophyll	KLOR oh fill	The chemical coloring (pigment) that makes plants look green. It is necessary for photosynthesis.
Cloud Forest	clowd FOR est	A rain forest in the cool, high mountains of the tropics. This forest is inhabited by many exotic plants, birds, and insects. The woods are often covered in mist.
Cone	kone	Woody, rounded structure that contains seeds. A pine cone has many seeds in it. Most trees with cones are evergreen, but the larch loses its needles each year.
Conifer	KONN ih fer	Trees that have cones with seeds, like pines, spruce, and hemlock. Almost all are evergreens.

Term	How to Say It	What It Means
Crown	krown	The leafy top of a tree.
Cultivated	KUL tih vaytid	Planted and cared for by people.
Cutting	KUT ing	A branch or twig cut from a tree that has grown roots.
Deciduous	de SID you us	Trees that lose all their leaves in the autumn—a botanist's term.
Defoliate	de FO lee ate	To cause all the leaves of a tree to fall off or be damaged. Disease or an infestation of insects can cause defoliation.
Entomologist	ento MOLL ah jist	A scientist who studies insects.
Evergreen	EVV er green	A tree that has green leaves on it all year long. Live oak and black spruce are both evergreens.
Family	FAM ill ee	A group of closely related trees. The Beech family includes many species, like American beech, bur oak, pin oak, and black oak.
Forest	FOR est	An extensive area covered with trees. A forest with most trees over 200 years old is called an old-growth forest, or virgin timberland.
Hardwood	HARD wood	Deciduous trees, or the lumber made from them, such as birch, maple, or oak. *Not* a scientific term.
Heartwood	HART wood	The wood at the center of a tree trunk, often much darker than the surrounding sapwood, as in the eastern red cedar.
Infestation	infess TAY shun	A large number of insects damaging a tree by eating its leaves or boring into the wood. An infestation of Gypsy moth caterpillars can completely defoliate a tree.
Larva Larvae (plural)	LAR va LAR vee	The young form of an insect. The larvae of some beetles tunnel into wood and bark.
Leaf Litter	leaf LIT ter	Layer of decaying leaves and twigs that cover the ground, especially in a forest.
Lichens	LYK ins	Small plants found on the trunk or branches of trees. Lichens are actually algae and fungi living together. Lichens are more abundant wherever there is little air pollution.

Term	How to Say It	What It Means
Native	NAY tive	Growing naturally wild. Scotch pine is native to Europe and Scandinavia, but it is cultivated all over North America.
Needles	NEE dlls	Long, thin leaves, like those of pine. Needles of spruce trees are short, but sharply pointed.
Non-native	non NAY tive	A tree that grows wild naturally in some other location or country—an alien species. Many trees found in nurseries are not native to that area.
Oxygen	OX ih jen	A gas produced by plants during photosynthesis. Animals need oxygen to live.
Petiole	PET ee ol	The stem of a leaf by which it is attached to the twig.
Photosynthesis	foto SIN the sis	Process by which plants combine water, carbon dioxide, and sunlight to make chlorophyll and oxygen.
Pigments	PIG ments	Chemicals which cause different colors.
Rain Forest	RAIN FOR est	A woodland with a very high annual rainfall, usually of at least 100 inches (250 cm). Most rain forests are in the tropics, although a few are in temperate climates. Most activity takes place in the forest canopy.
Riparian	ry PARE eeun	The banks of a river, the edge of a pond, stream, or lake. Willow, sycamore, and birch trees often grow in a **riparian habitat**.
Samara	sah MARR ah	The winged seeds of maples, elms, and ash trees.
Sapling	SAP ling	A young tree, less than 3 feet (1 m) tall. Saplings a few years old are often planted on Arbor Day or May Day.
Sapwood	SAP wood	The living, growing wood in the trunk of a tree. Often lighter in color than the heartwood.
Seedling	SEED ling	A sprouted tree seed—a very young tree. Seedlings about a foot tall are often sold by nurseries.

Term	How to Say It	What It Means
Shade Tree	shade tree	Trees planted along streets or near buildings for the shade they provide. Norway maple is often planted as a shade tree.
Softwood	SOFT wood	Pine, spruce, fir, and other conifers. Trees which produce a softer lumber than hardwoods do.
Shrub	shrub	A woody plant that usually has several main stems instead of a single trunk, and grows less than 15 feet (4.5 m) tall. Some shrubs do get to reach tree height.
Species	SPEE seez	A single type of tree, like the sugar maple. The Maple family includes over 100 species worldwide.
Timberline	TIM ber line	The location at the top of a mountain, or near the Arctic Circle, where trees stop growing.
Tree	tree	A large, woody plant with a single trunk, growing over 15 feet (4.5 m) tall. Usually with many branches, and living for many years.
Veins	vanes	The ribs and web-like lines on the blade of a leaf.

Index

acorns, 86, 88
ailanthus, 51, 52
alien species, 116–121
almond tree, 37, 88
amber, 25, 100
American arborvitae, 100, 101
American beech, 13, 17, 55, 77, 78, 88, 107
American desert, trees of, 65
American elm, 11, 54, 76
American holly, 92, 93
American longleaf pine, 23
American plum, 37
American sycamore, 20, 55
Antarctic Circle, 103, 104
ants, 80, 81
apple tree
  blossoms of, 23, 34, 35
  cultivation of, 33–34, 81, 83–84
  height of, 10
  Royal Gala, 84
Appleseed, Johnny, 84
Arbor Day, 42
arboretum, 53
arborvitae, American, 100, 101
Arctic Circle, 103, 104
ash
  European mountain, 56
  mountain, 11
  white, 56
aspen, 106
  big tooth (large-toothed), 41, 55, 74, 75
  quaking, 40, 55, 70, 75, 77, 103
  trembling, 45
aspirin, 66
autumn. *See* fall

balsam fir, 101
banana tree, 65
bark, 13, 80–81
basswood (linden), 49, 51
Bebb willow, 23, 40, 45, 55, 74, 75
beech, American, 13, 17, 55, 77, 78, 88, 107
Beech family, 19, 107. *See also specific family members*
beechnut, 88
beetles, 80, 81
Benjamin fig (*Benjamin ficus*), 105
berries, 90–91
bigtooth aspen, 41, 55, 74, 75
bigtooth maple, 54
birch
  black, 6, 20, 40
  canoe (*see* paper birch)
  cherry (*see* black birch)
  gray, 11, 55
  paper, 13, 20, 40, 55, 76, 88, 103, 107, 109
  sweet (*see* black birch), 20
  white (*see* paper birch)
  yellow, 40
Birch family, 13, 19, 40. *See also specific family members*
birds, 77, 89, 99, 110, 111
birthdays, planting trees on, 43
black birch, 20, 40
black cherry, 55
black gum. *See* Pepperidge
black locust, 56
black oak, 54, 62
black spruce (double spruce), 20, 103
black tupelo. *See* Pepperidge
black walnut, 84, 88
black willow, 11, 45, 55, 74, 75
blade, 12
blue gum, 113
blue paloverde, 65
blue spruce, 12, 95
bonsai trees, 105–106
botanical tree names, list of, 116–121
botanists, 17, 22, 115
box elder, 49, 51, 54
bracts, 31
Brazilian rubber tree, 64, 95
bristlecone pine, 25
broadleaf trees, 69
Buckeye family, 51. *See also specific family members*
buds, 107–111
butternut (white walnut), 56, 88
buttonwood, 20

cabbage palm, 64
cacao tree, 65
California fan palm (Washingtonia palm), 63
Canada plum tree, 37, 38
canoe birch. *See* paper birch
canyon live oak, 93
carbon dioxide, 15
cashew tree, 27
caterpillars, 47, 48, 49
catkins, 40, 41
cedar
  eastern red, 100, 101
  western red, 100
centipede, 80
Chapman, John, 84
cherry
  black, 55
  common choke-, 36, 37
  Japanese, 37
  pin, 37
  wild, 37
  wild black, 37
cherry birch, 20
cherry blossom festivals, 37
chestnut, horse, 51, 52
chlorophyll, 70
chocolate, 65
chokecherry, 36, 37
Christmas tree, 95
city street names, 49
climate, growth and, 23
cloud forest, 67
coconut palm, 64
collectors of leaves
  leaf identification cards for, 57–60
  leaf printmaking, 60–61
  notes for, 61
color change, of leaves, 69–76
common tree names, listing of, 116–121. *See also specific trees*
conifers, 97. *See also* Pine family
cork oak, 84
cottonwood, 40
  eastern, 74
crab apple tree, 37
Cretaceous period, 25
cricket, 80
crown, 9, 10
cultivation, 83–84, 113
cuttings, 45
cypress, 100

deciduous trees, 29, 68–70, 76, 77. *See also specific trees*
decorations, waxed-paper leaf, 104–105
defoliation, 48
desert, trees of, 65
dinosaur age, trees during, 25
dogwood, 31
  flowering, 31, 55, 77, 107, 108
  kousa, 31
  Pacific, 31
double spruce (black spruce), 20, 103
Douglas fir, 22, 25

eastern cottonwood, 74
eastern hemlock, 10, 11, 97, 100, 101
eastern red cedar, 100, 101
eastern redbud, 11, 43, 54
eastern white pine, 8, 21, 96, 97, 100, 103
elm, American, 11, 54, 76
Elm family, 19. *See also specific family members*
English oak, 106
English yew, 100, 101
entomologists, 115
eucalyptus, 105, 113
European mountain ash, 56
evergreen candles, 46
evergreens, 114. *See also specific trees*
  advantages of, 43–44
  needles of, 29
  new growth in, 46
  seedlings, 44
  in winter, 92–101

fall
  animal food from trees and, 88–91
  deciduous trees and, 68
  falling leaves and, 77–80

harvests of, 81–88
investigating bark in, 80–81
leaf color changes in, 69–76
photosynthesis and, 70, 73
families of trees, 17, 19, 116–121. *See also specific families*
Fiesta del Arbol, 42
fir, 10
balsam, 101
noble, 22
flax, 13
Florida royal palm, 64
flowering dogwood, 31, 55, 77, 107, 108
flowering trees, 31–41 *See also specific trees*
food, for wildlife, 88–91, 100
forest. *See also specific trees*
cloud, 67
future and, 115
protection of, 115
rain, 67
tree flowers of, 37
foresters, 17
forestry work, 115
fossil leaves, 25
fruit trees, 63, 84

ghost gum, 105. *See also* eucalyptus
giant saguaro, 66
giant sequoia, 22, 100
ginkgo, 24, 25, 52
glossary of tree terms, 122–125
grain pattern, 15
gray birch, 11, 55
great horned owl, 99
growing cycles, 22
growth
climate and soil conditions for, 23
evergreen candles, 46
new, 46
records for, 22
rings, 13–15
starting tree from cuttings, 45
Gypsy moth caterpillars, 48

hackmatack, 20
hardwoods, 69
harvest, fall, 81–88
hawthorn, 34, 91, 107, 108
scarlet, 55
heartwood, 13, 15
height of trees, record setters for, 22
hemlock
eastern, 10, 11, 97, 100, 101
western, 22, 25
hemlock loopers, 48
hickory
pignut, 56
shagbark, 56, 81, 87, 88
hiking trails, 53
holly, American, 92, 93
Holly family, 93
horn pine. *See* Pepperidge
horse chestnut trees, 51, 52

identification tags, 108, 111
incense cedar, 22
India rubber tree, 105, 106
indoor forests, 105–106
infestation, 48
insects, 47–49, 80–81
ironbark tree, 113

jack pine, 97
Jersey pine, 20
Joshua tree, 65
juniper, 100

karri, 108
Kilmer, Alfred Joyce (*Trees*), 22, 52
kola, 34
kousa dogwood, 31

landscaping evergreens, 100
larch (tamarack), 20, 113
latex, 95
Laurel family, 25. *See also specific family members*
leaf/leaves, 10–12
color changes in fall, 69–70, 77
falling, 77–80
identification cards, making, 57–60
litter, 77, 79–80
miners, 48
number from one tree, 73
parts of, 12
prints, making, 60–62
separation from tree, 70
summer, identifying, 53–62
veins, 12
waxed-paper, 104–105
lichens, 81, 82
light, 15
lime tree, 67
linden (basswood), 49, 51
live oak, 54, 93, 103
locust, black, 56
longleaf pine, 97
American, 23

magnolia
saucer, 32
southern, 31, 92, 93
Magnolia family, 31. *See also specific family members*
maple
bigtooth (large-toothed), 54
northern, 37
Norway, 49, 51, 54, 72
red, 10, 37, 39, 49, 54, 70, 72, 73, 110
silver, 49, 50
sugar, 11, 29, 30, 37, 54, 70, 71, 72
Maple family. *See also specific family members*
color changes of, 73–74
leaves of, 19, 25, 72
seeds or samaras of, 23, 59, 71, 72, 88
shape of trees, 10
maple syrup, making, 28–30
mast, 88
Methuselah, 25
millipedes, 80
moths, 49, 81
mountain ash, 11
mugho pine, 95
mulberry, white, 54
museum, 53

names of trees
common, 20, 116–121
scientific (botanical), 22
native, 20
nature centers, 53
new growth, evidence of, 46
news, trees in, 63
noble fir, 22
Norfolk pine, 93, 105
North Pole, 103–104
northern catalpa, 51, 54
northern maple flower, 37
northern red oak, 76
Norway maple, 49, 51, 54, 72
Norway spruce, 95
nut trees, 84–88
nutrients, 17

oak, 23, 37
black, 54, 62
canyon live, 93
cork, 84
English, 106
live, 54, 93, 103
northern red, 76
pin, 49, 54
red, 15
swamp white, 54
white, 11, 30, 54
Ohio buckeye, 51, 56

oldest living trees, 25–26
orange tree, 84, 93
osage orange tree, 40
ovenbird, 77
oxygen, 15

Pacific dogwood, 31
Pacific willow, 45
Pacific yew, 63, 100
paleobotanist, 25
palm trees, 63–64
cabbage, 64
California fan, 63
coconut, 64
Florida royal, 64
sabal palmetto, 64
Washingtonia, 63
paloverde
blue, 65
yellow, 65
paper, 114
paper birch
bark of, 13, 107, 109
catkins of, 40
cold temperatures and, 103
common names for, 20
leaves of, 55, 76
range of, 76
seeds of, 88
park rangers, 17, 18
parks, 53
peach tree, 37, 84
pear tree, 37
pecan tree, 84
Pepperidge, 20, 70, 77
petiole, 12, 74
photosynthesis, 17, 70, 73
pignut hickory, 56
pin cherry, 37
pin oak, 49, 54
pine. *See also* fir, hemlock, spruce
American longleaf, 23
bristlecone, 25
eastern white, 8, 21, 96, 97, 100, 103
horn. *See* Pepperidge
Jersey, 20
longleaf, 97
mugho, 95
Norfolk, 93, 105
pitch, 11, 96, 97, 100
Ponderosa, 22
Scotch, 95, 100, 101
scrub, 20
sugar, 97
Virginia, 20
white, 15, 96
pinecones, 97
Pine family, 19, 94–99, 103. *See also specific family members*
pine needles, 96–97
pine seedling, 112
pistachio tree, 27
pitch pine, 11, 96, 97, 100

planetree, 20
planting a tree, 42–43
plum tree, 37
  Canada, 37, 38
poison sumac, 27
Ponderosa pine, 22
poplar, yellow. *See* tulip tree
protection of forests, 115
pussy willow, 40

quaking aspens
  catkins of, 40
  cold temperatures and, 103
  leaves of, 55, 70, 74, 75, 77

rain forests, 67
rayon, 37
recycling, 114
redbud, 11, 43, 54
red cedar, eastern, 100, 101
red gum tree (eucalyptus), 105, 113
red maple, 49, 110
  flowers of, 37, 39
  leaves of, 54, 70, 72, 73
  shape of, 10
red oak, 15
red pine, 97
redwood, 22, 100, 115
riparian habitat, 67
river bank, trees on, 67
roots, 9, 10
Rose family, 19, 33–37
Royal Gala apples, 84
rubber tree, Brazilian, 64, 95
rubber tree plant, India, 105, 106

sabal palmetto palm, 64
saguaro cactus, 66
samaras, 23, 59, 71, 72, 88
sapling, 42
sapwood, 13–14
sassafras, 55, 73, 76
saucer magnolia, 32
sawflies, 48
scarlet hawthorn, 55
scientific names of trees, 22
Scotch pine, 95, 100, 101
scrub pine, 20
seedlings, evergreen, 44
seeds, 23. *See also* samaras *and specific nuts*
sequoia, giant, 22, 100
serviceberry (shadbush), 11, 34, 55
shadbush (serviceberry), 11, 34, 55
shade trees, 49
shagbark hickory, 56, 81, 87, 88
shapes of leaves, 10–11
shapes of trees, 10
shelter, for wildlife, 100
shrubs or bushes, 9–10
silver dollar gum (eucalyptus), 105, 113
silver maple, 49, 50
Sitka spruce, 22, 25
snail, 80
soil conditions, for growth, 23
sour gum. *See* Pepperidge
South Pole, 103–104
southern magnolia, 31, 92, 93
sowbug, 80
species, of tree, 17, 19–20. *See also specific species*
spider, 80
spring
  celebration of, 42–45
  evidence of new growth and, 46
  flowering trees and, 31–41
  maple syrup making and, 28–30
spruce, 10
  black (double spruce), 20, 95, 103
  blue, 12, 95
  Norway, 95
  Sitka, 22, 25
  white, 95
squirrels, 100
staghorn sumac, 76, 90
street names, 49, 106
stringybark, 105. *See also* eucalyptus tree
sugar maple, 29, 54, 71, 72
  flower of, 37
  leaves of, 11, 30, 70
sugar pine, 97
sugarhouse (sugar shack), 29–30
sumac
  poison, 27
  staghorn, 76, 90
Sumac family, 27
summer
  battle against bugs, 47–49
  identifying leaves in, 53–62
  scouting for trees, 49–53
  trees from around the world, 63–67
swamp white oak, 54
sweet birch, 20
sweet gum, 55, 73, 76
sycamore
  American, 20, 55
  bark, 107

tamarack (larch), 20, 113
temperate rain forest, 67
temperatures, cold, 93
  leaf color change and, 70
  tree survival in, 102–104
tent caterpillars, 48
tick, 80
tiger swallowtail butterfly, 47
timber workers, 23
timberline, 104
town trees, 49–52
tree of heaven, 51
trees. *See also specific trees or tree families*
  families listing, 116–121
  form and shape, 10
  future and, 115
  mature, 23
  parts of, 9, 10
  photosynthesis and, 15–17
  products from, 114
  protection of, 115
  as resource for people, 113–114
  science of, 17–22
  study of, 17
  terms, 122–125
  what are, 9–10
tree watcher's notebook, 57
trembling aspen, 45
Triassic period, 25
trips, tips for, 53
tropical rain forest, 67, 114
trunk, 9, 10, 13
tulip tree, 11, 20, 33, 76, 88
tupelo, black. *See* Pepperidge

Virginia pine, 20

walnut
  black, 84, 88
  white (butternut tree), 56, 88
Walnut family, 19
Washingtonia palm (California fan palm), 63
water, 16, 17, 43
waxed-paper leaves, 104–105
weeping willow, 40, 45, 70
western hemlock, 22, 25
western red cedar, 100
white ash, 56
white birch. *See* paper birch
white mulberry, 54
white oak, 11, 30, 54
white pine, 15, 96
  pine, eastern, 8, 21, 96, 97, 100, 103
white spruce, 103
white walnut (butternut tree), 56, 88
wild black cherry, 37
wildlife
  food for, 88–91, 100
  in leaf litter, 77
  shelter for, 100
willow. *See also* aspen
  Bebb, 23, 40, 45, 55, 74, 75
  black, 11, 45, 55, 74, 75
  Pacific, 45
  weeping, 40, 45, 70
Willow family, 25, 45
  bark of, 66
  buds of, 107
  catkins, 40
  fall leaf color changes, 74–76
  seeds of, 60
  species, 19
winter
  activities for, 104–106
  buds, 107–111
  evergreens in, 92–101. *See also* evergreens
  tree survival in cold temperatures, 102–104
wood, 13–15, 114
woodcutters, 23
woodlands. *See* forests

yellow birch catkins, 40
yellow paloverde, 65
yellow poplar. *See* tulip tree
yew, 88
  English, 100, 101
  Pacific, 63, 100